Swing to Flow

A Mindful Approach to Better Golf

Revised and Expanded Edition

by

Steve A. Furman

Table of Contents

Copyright

Title: Swing to Flow: A Mindful Approach to Better Golf: Revised and Expanded Edition

Author: Steve A. Furman, Publisher: Steve A. Furman, Cover Design: Steve A. Furman

ISBN (Paperback): 979-8-9999138-3-8 First Edition March 2026

swingtoflow.com

What's New in this Edition

Swing to Flow: A Mindful Approach to Better Golf was first published in November 2025 as both a paperback and an eBook. I also launched **swingtoflow.com** as a companion site, knowing there would be more about the Swing to Flow approach I wanted to share going forward.

After publication, it became clear that some key concepts deserved deeper exploration—and needed to further clarification.

I added new sections: **Commitment, Flipping the Switch** and **The Motion is the Memory**—that explores the neuroscience behind how mind and body work together. It explains how the golf swing is captured in the brain and where it resides, deepening understanding of why the *Swing to Flow* model works.

I significantly revised the **Flow Score** sections and introduced the **Flow Index**—a new dimension that, when paired with stroke totals, offers players more ways to analyze their play and track genuine improvement.

The beginner chapter has been renamed **New Player? Start at the Hole, Not the Tee** and includes a completely revised approach I believe will be more valuable to those just starting out.

Many other sections have been updated or clarified for smoother reading and sharper insights. Some content has been deleted due to redundancy, and some content has been given its own section. A comprehensive glossary was added as well.

If you purchased the original edition and are reading this, thank you for your support. It means a lot. I hope you find this edition helpful in your quest to improve your play as well as your enjoyment of the game.

For additional content, updates, and the downloadable Flow Scorecard, visit **swingtoflow.com**.

Preface

I remember the moment I decided I wanted to be a golfer. I was thirteen, just a normal kid in Springfield, Illinois, surrounded by endless cornfields and looking for something bigger than my small world.

Our town had a few municipal golf courses, and whenever we drove past one in our Pontiac Tempest station wagon, I'd press my face against the back window and stare. The grass looked impossibly green. Foursomes walked the fairways in quiet concentration, unhurried and purposeful. They looked serene in a way that resonated with me. I wanted that. I wanted to be one of them.

I started watching every golf tournament on TV—which wasn't many in those days, mostly the major championships like the Masters and the U.S. Open. Golf seemed like a sport I could actually do. My body wasn't built for contact sports, but golf? Golf was different. Golf was possibility.

I scrounged up a couple of second-hand clubs, strapped them to my bike, and rode two miles to the Bergen Park Golf Course. It was a modest 9-hole municipal course, but to me it might as well have been Augusta National. I'd walk the edges looking for lost balls, building my collection one scuffed Titleist at a time.

But I needed to practice. When it was time to mow the lawn at home, I'd lower the blade on the mower and carve out a makeshift green in the backyard. Soon I was chipping short irons onto the green and pretending to be playing against Jack Nicklaus. My confidence grew, and so I set up a tee box in the front yard and started hitting balls over our one-story house to that bespoke green in the back corner of the yard.

4

One afternoon, I walked around the house to find one of my shots resting in the hole. My first hole-in-one! I stood there with a wide grin on my face. I'd been bitten by the golf bug. There was no turning back.

Whenever I had money in my pocket, I was off to Bergen Park. I borrowed every golf book our library had—*How to Play Your Best Golf All the Time* by Tommy Armourbecame my sacred text—and filled notebooks with swing thoughts and tips. I documented everything: what worked, what didn't, which adjustments helped, which made things worse. I was teaching myself the game from the ground up, one page and one round at a time. [1]

When it came time for college, I chose psychology as my major. I was particularly drawn to experimental psychology, statistics, and physiological psychology—what we now call biopsychology, the mind-body connection. I didn't know it then, but I was learning something that would later prove to be an essential part of my golf game.

Meanwhile, I kept working on my swing. But as every golfer knows, understanding mechanics intellectually and applying them under pressure are two very different things. After years of practice and play, I hit a wall. My game got stuck—one step forward, one back. The pattern repeated endlessly. It was maddening.

In my thirties, I discovered Buddhism. I'd always been searching for ways to sharpen my mental focus, and Buddhist meditation offered exactly that. The practice became a daily discipline—not as religion, but as a practical method for training my mind. Over decades, it became my mental foundation, an ever-present resource for managing distraction and intrusion, whether at home, at work, or standing over a three-foot putt.

Then came another insight, this time from my career. I'd spent twenty years leading digital customer experience at a Fortune 500 company. My job was studying how people make decisions, learn new skills, and perform under pressure. I helped millions of customers navigate unfamiliar digital experiences by understanding not just *what* they did, but *why* they did it—and *how to make complex tasks intuitive.*

One day it hit me: I'd been solving this exact problem professionally for two decades. I'd successfully applied behavioral insights to help people master complicated digital systems. Why couldn't I apply the same approach to golf?

It would take years before I fully understood how meditation had transformed the way I played. I'd learned the mechanics. I'd practiced hundreds of hours. I knew what I was supposed to do and could do it. But meditation taught me something deeper—how to let intuition be my guide. How to stop trying to control every variable. How to trust the swing I'd built without fear or overthinking. How to be completely present in the moment without anticipation of what came next.

Golf became where everything converged—my decades of playing, my understanding of human behavior, my meditation practice. It became my laboratory for testing what I'd learned about focus, presence, and intuition.

The Question That Changed Everything

What if there was a way to integrate golf's mechanical fundamentals with natural intuitive intelligence—that deeper knowing that exists beyond analysis and overthinking?

This question drove me to create and develop the *Swing to Flow* process, which recognizes golf as both a physical skill and a form of moving meditation. Peak performance emerges when we combine thorough preparation with complete presence in the moment. It was a game changer for me.

My hope is that it helps you unlock your full potential on the course.

The Missing Element in Golf Instruction

Early golf instruction focused almost entirely on swing mechanics. Alex Morrison's *A New Way to Better Golf* (1933) built his entire approach around what he called: "The inescapable mechanical and anatomical factors that govern successful shots." While Morrison acknowledged the importance of feeling the swing and devoted space to muscle memory (more on that term later), he never addresses the mind's role during play. Despite being an exceptional ball striker who toured the country showcasing his skills, Morrison seems to have left the mental game unexplored.[2]

Ben Hogan's *Five Lessons: The Modern Fundamentals of Golf* (1957)—widely regarded as golf's original bible—is pure mechanics. Hogan demystifies the swing's complexity with deceptively simple language accompanied by clear illustrations. But he never reveals the mental approach that made him an icon. Hogan famously isolated himself during tournaments, keeping competitors at arm's length. Perhaps that's why he showed us the Hogan swing but never the Hogan mind.

Harvey Penick's Little Red Book, Lessons and Teachings from a Lifetime in Golf (1992) is a gem. Penick spent his entire life playing and teaching golf in Austin—thirty-three years as golf coach at the University of Texas, fifty years as head professional at the Austin Country Club. Late in life, he decided to share the personal notes he'd kept private for decades. I've returned to his book countless times.

His diary focuses on golf mechanics, yet it's packed with practical wisdom that cuts through technical jargon of the swing. Despite these insights, Penick never fully addresses how a player might develop the mental side of the game. You get stories and keen observations, but no systematic approach to the mind.

Take his comment on putting: "Once you adopt a good system for putting, the rest of it is mental. Stay with your system." He understood that the mental game was an essential component, but he didn't tell us how to master it.[3]

Jack Nicklaus knew the value of the mental game. His book *Golf My Way* (1974), written with Ken Bowden, and *My Golf Lessons: 100-Plus Ways to Improve Your Shots, Lower Scores and Enjoy Golf Much, Much More* (2002), dedicated significant sections to visualization and mental preparation. "I never hit a shot, not even in practice, without having a very sharp in-focus picture of it in my head."[4]

Although everyone wants to play like Jack, instruction remains a mechanics-first approach, despite mounting evidence about the mind's critical role in peak performance. There are excellent books and digital content related to exploring the mental game, but I believe they are overshadowed by mechanics and equipment. Watch any PGA tournament broadcast: commercials overflow with the latest golf ball, or a new driver. The latest devices are launch monitors and simulators. If you are a recreational player, the message is: only equipment, tips, lessons, and range time are the way to go.

Fitted clubs, professional instruction, and mechanical practice enhanced with stats from monitors are important and extremely helpful. I use this technology myself to see both the visual impact, as well as the wealth of data it generates.

Working with a PGA professional is enlightening, but most amateurs don't pursue this path. Cost and availability play roles, but I believe there's something deeper. The vast majority of recreational golfers play between 12 and 20 rounds per year. They don't seek tournament competition—they simply want to enjoy the game with friends or family, but don't want to be the weakest player in the group.[5]

Today's players increasingly turn to online instruction—free, endless and filled with promises of "quick fixes." This wealth of content overwhelmingly focuses on mechanics, while largely ignoring the consciousness guiding the club. This misses what captivated me about golf—those effortless moments when my best shots seem to happen out of thin air.

I joined a golf forum as a research project and began posting about the mental game. One of the moderators and I exchanged messages, and his position was clear: "The mental game, 'is only a tiny fraction of the game and in what determines the quality of a shot.' He was solely focused on mechanics, posting detailed images of his swing. Here's what that perspective overlooks. The mental aspects of your game and mechanics practice are both forms of preparation that directly influence performance. Both are critical. The difference is you can't practice your swing while playing, but you can use your mind throughout your round. Most of your time on the course is spent between shots, not swinging a club. Use that time wisely.

My Personal Transformation

Since I embraced these principles, golf has become far more enjoyable and has helped me lower my handicap. I can now access my highest potential more frequently, and believe this framework can help lots of players experience both a more profound connection to the game and better score outcomes.

Introduction

If you're reading this, you're part of an exciting moment in the history of golf. The National Golf Foundation reported a remarkable 40% increase in participation among Americans in 2023, driven by everything from traditional courses to off-course options like Topgolf, driving ranges, and simulators. More people are discovering golf than ever before. In 2024—the latest year stats were available at the time of writing this book—the number of rounds played exceeded 531 million.[6]

But here's what the statistics don't reveal: How many of those new players will still be playing in five years? How many will fall in love with the game versus walking away frustrated? And perhaps most importantly—how many will experience the deeper satisfaction that comes from genuine improvement?

Growth in participation doesn't automatically translate to growth in mastery or enjoyment. Too many golfers—new and experienced alike—struggle with the same challenges: inconsistent ball-striking, frustrating scores, and the nagging sense that they should be playing better than they are. The game that at times promises so much often delivers frustration instead.

This book offers a different way to approach your golf experience. It's not for everyone, but if you've ever felt stuck despite putting in the work, it's a small investment that could change the way you think about your game.

The *Swing to Flow* framework you're about to learn isn't built on complicated swing theories or endless technical adjustments. It's built on something more fundamental: understanding how your mind and body work together to produce great golf. When you align your analytical (mechanics) preparation with intuitive (mental) execution—when you learn to separate thinking from doing—the game can transform from a battle against mechanics into a partnership with consciousness.

That's what the Swing to Flow process is. A way of approaching golf that awakens your natural abilities.

According to Golf Digest, more than 10,000 English-language golf books have been published. When considering books in all languages, historical works, and the modern self-publishing boom, the total is likely significantly higher.[7]

The earliest publication of a book I could find written about golf is actually a poem: *Glotta* by James Arbuckle (1721)[8] who was a student at the University of Glasgow. The Scottish Golf History website has a list of other notable books from the 1800.[9]

Yet for all these thousands of books, many of which are instructional, most players struggle with the same fundamental mystery: why do I play brilliantly one day and poorly the next?

The Golfing Machine

One day in 1939, Homer Kelley, an engineer at Boeing, living in Tacoma, Washington, was asked by his boss if he wanted to play a round of golf at the Meadow Park Municipal Golf Course. He had never played before but thought, "How hard can it be?" Off they went. At the round's end Kelley shot a 116.

He did not play again for six months, until his co-workers coaxed him out again. They played Highland Golf Course—slightly tougher than Meadow Park. He finished with a 77. He had no idea how he could shoot that low score but was determined to find out. He worked with several pros, searching for answers to that question. Mostly they said he must have been very relaxed that day. Kelley was not satisfied with that answer; he wanted a full understanding.[10]

After thirty years and thousands of hours of personal discovery hitting balls in his garage, Kelley painstakingly documented the technical details of the golf swing. He introduced his revolutionary approach to golf, *The Golfing Machine*, in 1969. He called it *The STAR System; Geometric Golf: The Computer Age Approach to Golfing Perfection*. It's an exhaustive work that attempts to explain the golf swing by understanding force, motion, geometry, structure and pattern development. It is not an attempt to simplify golf. He says, "Demanding that golf instruction be kept simple does not make it simple—only incomplete and ineffective."[11]

In his book, Kelley writes, "An invaluable ally is the computer. This is a built-in analyzer that everyone seems to have, though few are aware of it and even fewer use it, and almost none of those use it consciously. It's a mysterious subconsciousness process that conscious thought only annoys." I interpret his term "computer" to be the *mind*.[12]

This is classic Kelley—his engineering background showing through every word. But here's the irony: in his own mechanical way, he's making my exact point. This *mysterious subconscious process* he describes? That's our mental game. And according to Kelley, conscious thought only gets in its way. This is a critical point to recognize. The mechanics savant is saying the mental game isn't just important to playing better golf—it's *the* game of golf.

Kelley was right, the mental game isn't workable through engineering. But the mental game was never meant to be engineered. It was meant to be, cultivated, trusted and put to use while playing—alongside mechanics. That's what he missed.

His book has been revised several times since publication and you can obtain a copy for yourself online. Be warned: it reads like an instruction manual for how a jet engine operates. But if you take the time, it's full of fantastic insights. Despite being perhaps the ultimate mechanics handbook on the swing, it remains largely unknown.

Kelley's obsession with mechanical perfection mirrors today's dominant approach to golf instruction. Most instructors focus on swing mechanics during lessons. You leave feeling prepared and confident, expecting better performance. You may see brief improvement, but it fades, and disappointment returns.

Modern golf studios like Golf-Tec take things further, using cameras and sensors to capture swing data. My five-lesson experience in 2019 with Golf-Tec was highly beneficial. Six years later, I can still log on to their portal and see the videos and stats from those sessions. I learned a lot about the mechanics of my swing as well as getting valuable feedback on my putting stance. While these technology tools advance our understanding of golf physics, knowing launch angle and spin rate mean little when standing on the first tee with racing heart and cluttered mind.

Instructors love sharing success stories—clients who gained 20 yards off the tee after just a few sessions. These stories, whether true or not, primarily serve to sell more lessons to struggling golfers desperate for quick fixes. We all cling to the belief that discovering one crucial adjustment will permanently unlock our perfect swing.

But here's what most golfers experience: You can understand numerous technical details, make a perfect swing on the range, and still find yourself helpless when it matters most. You know what to do, but you can't seem to access that mechanical knowledge when you need it. Your body tenses, thoughts spin, and the smooth swing you had in practice evaporates under the pressure of course play.

Swing to Flow provides a framework for improving the quality of awareness you bring to each shot. You'll learn to quiet your analytical mind that interferes with your body's natural intelligence, and access the intuitive state where your best golf lives—the same at ease awareness Homer Kelley experienced when he shot a 77. The pros who told him he must have been really relaxed that day were right. They just lacked the vocabulary to explain why and how to do it.

Most golf instructors don't actively teach the mental game—not because they doubt its importance, but because it's difficult to explain and teach. Physical instruction is tangible: Do this with your right arm, and your swing will find the tour slot like the pros. Concepts like mindfulness and flow states don't easily translate into lesson plans or compelling sales pitches—those are left to the sports psychologists.

This book is for any golfer ready to strengthen their mental game—whether you're experienced but frustrated, or new and want to build the right foundation. Rather than another swing manual, you'll get a systematic process for accessing the power of your mind: trusting instincts, entering flow states, and playing with mindful awareness instead of mechanical overthinking.

Before we dig in, Let's look at what makes golf so challenging.

Superpowers Required

The more you know about the mechanics of the game—or think you do—the more challenging it becomes to play well. It's counterintuitive. This is golf's cruelest paradox: mechanics knowledge becomes a burden.

The beginner who knows nothing might swing freely and make solid contact, while a golfer who has studied swing planes, weight shift, and impact positions finds himself paralyzed on the first tee.

During a round, you encounter various obstacles: different lies, grasses, slopes, sand traps, and even those sneaky greenskeepers who cut holes like it's the final round of The Masters. And of course, there's the weather. Each situation demands constant analytical recalibration.

You need to resolve the proper grip, stance, ball placement, alignment to the target and much more. All these details must be seamlessly integrated and automatic. It requires the ability to be laser-focused amidst multiple distractions and maintain a level of concentration that lies between overthinking and underthinking—a state of awareness where the body's natural intelligence can operate freely.

Golfers use a diverse range of clubs. Most sports require mastering just one piece of equipment. This alone makes golf more complex.

The rules of golf allow up to fourteen clubs in the bag. It sounds like a lot, or maybe too many. Who really knows? They have multiple shapes, lengths and lofts, and you must make adjustments based on the club being used. It's uncommon to use the same club on consecutive shots—except for the putter—and some clubs may never be used or used only once during a round. This constant adaptation tests both your technical skills and mental agility.

Consider the difference between golf and other sports. A professional baseball player must react in a split-second to a pitch thrown over 95 mph, a ball hit toward them, or a situation on the bases. They possess elite real-time decision-making skills, and there's no time for contemplation. Surprisingly, having no thinking time makes it easier to react. Their minds know what to do and their bodies can do it—analytical interference only disrupts the process.

Golf is a completely different experience. The ball just sits there taunting you, the course masquerades as an idyllic, peaceful pasture, and the hole is really, really small. Your challenger is not another person—it's you. You're all alone, playing a solitary game with nothing but time to think, plan, worry, and second-guess. This thinking time, which may seem like an advantage, becomes your greatest enemy. Start analyzing and adjusting your swing mid-round and focus shatters.

Thinking time on the course is where Swing to Flow lives. If you play for four hours and shoot a 95, you spent roughly 1% of that time actually swinging a club. The other ninety-nine percent? You spent it thinking. What you're thinking about during that time determines your mental state—and your mental state shapes every shot.

A round of golf may appear to be a relaxing walk in nature, but it's actually an exhausting internal battle against distractions. Watching a few minutes of a PGA tournament, we see elite golfers swing a club in an almost effortless manner and think, "It can't be that hard." You know better. You always play outdoors, and it lasts for hours. There's only one member on your team, and there's no stepping off the course to rest while someone else continues the round. The swing begins and your hands go from completely still to 80 or 90+ mph in less than two seconds, abruptly changing directions halfway through.

The golf swing is a highly complex athletic movement that activates muscle groups throughout the entire body—from the feet and legs through the core, back, chest, shoulders, and arms—while coordinating movement across all major joints in a precise kinetic sequence. This is why golf is also an intense physical activity demanding considerable strength and coordination despite appearing to be a precision sport.[13]

Golf requires superpowers. While physical strength is welcome, the ability to block distractions, trust the mind, and access a state of effortless concentration are the true skills you need. If you can occupy a state of mindfulness, a place that allows knowledge to serve rather than hinder, where the conscious mind steps aside allowing your intuitive wisdom to emerge, you're on the Swing to Flow path.

Let's begin.

The Swing to Flow Process

Most golfers eventually hit a plateau. They play for several years and improve. Take lessons and they move up a notch or two. Over time their handicap improves—then stalls. Bright spots appear in each round, but the ability to string together quality shot after quality shot remains elusive. The dreaded double-bogey pops up, turning what might have been a best round into something very familiar.

Why?

Golfers tend to double down on what isn't working—more lessons, more range time, more mechanical fixes. But the problem may not be their swing. *Golfers keep trying to fix their swing when what they really need to fix is their relationship with the swing they already have.*

Playing eighteen holes of good golf requires dozens of solid back-to-back shots, sound decisions, and the discipline to keep emotions in check. After a poor round, the spontaneous reaction is to head back to the range, pound balls, and perhaps search for more tips online. We're looking for what we're doing wrong, or not doing, in hopes of finding that "fix." There is a show on The Golf Channel called The Golf Fix. Nothing wrong with that, but many of golf's challenges aren't mechanical problems requiring mechanical solutions—they're consciousness problems that require consciousness solutions.

Range practice is important but not enough, because the range doesn't recreate the mental demands of actual play. You can perform a perfect swing in the isolated environment of practice, but if you can't access that swing when it matters, that perfect practice swing is immaterial.

The Three Skills of Golf

Most golfers work endlessly on their swing and wonder why they don't improve their score. The reason: they're developing only one of golf's three essential skills. These are the Swing to Flow core essentials of golf.

1. Learn How to Swing

Learn the physical laws that govern solid contact. Develop techniques: full and partial swings, bunker shots, chipping and putting skills. You're encoding these swings as learned response patterns inside the circuits of your brain. This is your **intuitive mind**: procedural memory. The part that runs the swing. (See The Motion is the Memory)

2. Learn How to Play

Learn to navigate the golf course effectively: club choice, course management, recovery shots. This is your **analytical mind**: declarative memory. It's the thinking part. The preparation between and just before you make a shot.

3. Learn How to Switch Minds

Learn how to transition from analytical mind to intuitive mind during play. This is the mental game—the skill most golfers never develop. It's what allows preparation to become execution: quieting the analytical mind, trusting procedural memory, and committing fully to each shot.

Understanding these three skills is the first step. Developing all three of these skills is another. So let's look at what golfers actually do.

The Mental Game Gap

I've asked hundreds of golfers over the years if they work on their mental game. The vast majority of their answers fall into one of three camps. Either, "I work on it all the time," "I want to," or "what's the mental game?"

When I ask camp one to explain, they rattle off a list of mechanics: ball position, backswing, grip, etc. They are trying to improve with mechanics alone, and believe thinking about mechanics is the same as their mental game. This reveals a fundamental misunderstanding—*thinking about swing mechanics isn't mental practice, it's mechanical practice happening in your head.*

When I dig deeper with camp two, they typically talk about focus or concentration, but struggle to explain what those terms mean. They don't have a clearly defined mental process and are focused on outcomes rather than the inner conditions that can unlock better swings.

The third group—players who have no idea that golf involves mental skills—are just trying to hit the ball as far as they can. We'll leave it at that.

Of the players who claim to work on their mental game, I ask them to quantify the ratio of their mechanics practice to mental practice. This is what most of them tell me: 90% mechanics, 10% mental. I'm skeptical.

What is your ratio of mechanics practice to mental practice? Let's find out.

Try this exercise. Grab a piece of paper and draw a vertical line down the middle. Label one column "Mechanics" and the other "Mental." Now list the things you practice in each category.

Take your time. Be honest.

If you're like most golfers, the mechanics column filled up quickly. Grip. Stance. Backswing. Weight transfer. Follow-through. Chipping from tight lies. Putting. You've worked on these things for years—on the range, in lessons, through videos and tips. You know what mechanics practice looks like.

The mental column is probably shorter. Maybe much shorter. Maybe empty.

If you're happy with your game and playing experience is improving to your satisfaction, there's no need to read further. If not, and you're looking to play more consistently and get more enjoyment from golf, keep reading.

If you haven't intentionally been developing your mental skills, you're leaving strokes on the course. You already have a mental game—it's just untrained. The Swing to Flow process offers a systematic way to make it available when you need it most.

Three Interconnected Elements

The three skills—**swinging**, **playing**, and **switching**—form the Swing to Flow foundation. But to truly master them, we need to understand the underlying elements and how they work together.

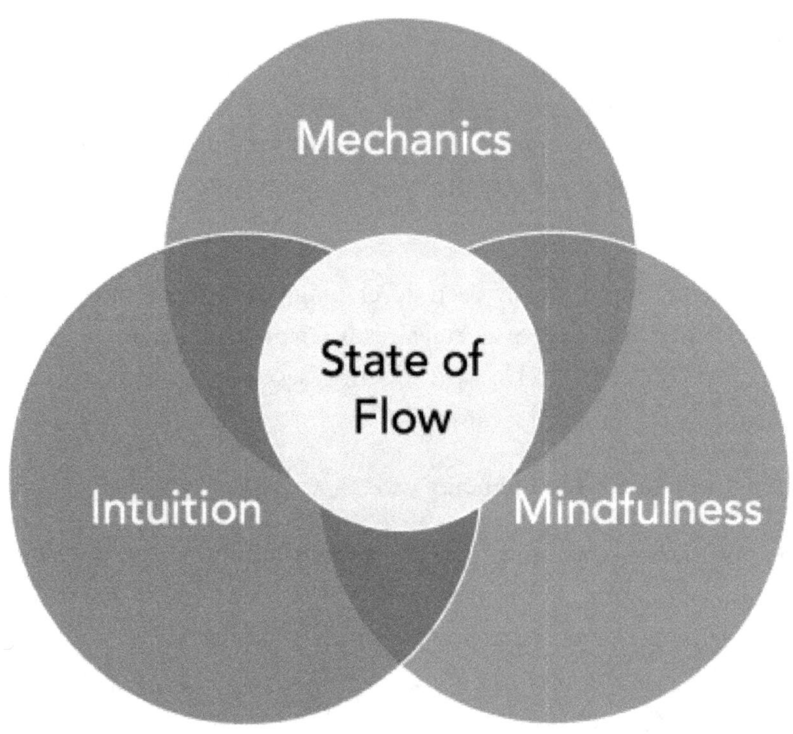

The process consists of: your **Mechanics**, your **Mindfulness**, and your **Intuition**. They aren't separate—they overlap and enhance each other.

Let's dive deeper.

Mechanics are the skills you develop through sound technique and practice. **Mindfulness** is the ability to focus on the present moment while calmly acknowledging thoughts without judgment. **Intuition** is the ability to know something instantly without conscious reasoning and allowing that intuition to run the swing.

When all three elements align, you can enter the center space—**State of**

Flow, where pure swings emerge naturally. In this state your swing feels effortless and flows without conscious thought, because you're fully absorbed in the present moment.

The power of this model lies in its flexibility: you don't need to perfect all three elements before seeing results. You can enter through any element and realize improvement.

Throughout this book, we'll explore each element in depth and, more importantly, how to develop an integrated approach. The goal isn't perfection in any single element but rather the harmonious integration of all three—the pathway to flow.

At the highest level, peak performance becomes sustainable when all three elements align. They create a synergy—producing performance that exceeds what any single element could achieve alone.

Mechanics

Solid fundamentals form the foundation of consistent golf. You must understand what creates an effective swing and develop the physical skills to repeat it reliably. Technique and deliberate practice sessions are a given. Without sound mechanics, every other aspect of your game lacks a stable base.

A Self-Sustaining Cycle

Here's what makes the Swing to Flow process effective. A solid **mechanical** foundation frees your mind from worrying about your swing, creating space for mindful presence. **Mindful** presence creates calm that allows the analytical mind to clearly think through situations and allows intuition to lead the swing. Trusting **intuition** allows your fluid motion to appear, opening space for flow. **Flow** renews motivation to practice and deepens engagement.

Think of those shots when your swing felt effortless and you launched the ball at the target. You striped it, or flushed it; whatever term you want to use. If you make that motion—the one that results in dead perfect contact four or five times during a round and have an open mind to new ideas—Swing to Flow is made for you.

Those effortless shots prove you already possess the necessary mechanics—*what you're missing is reliable access to the mental state that produces them.* Imagine making pure contact twenty or twenty-five times a round. That heightened mental state is transformative. It greatly enriches your enjoyment and, as Bobby Jones said, helps you experience the real pleasure in golf: "not the score but the execution of shots." While there are no guarantees about lower scores, investing time to internalize these principles will result in positive changes.

Best of all, it works with the swing you already have by adding mental mastery that unlocks more consistent access to your best golf. You're not starting over—you're adding to what you've already built. Think of it as a scaffold. You build it one level at a time, placing a solid footing atop each section so it can continue to rise.

Before we explore the three key elements of the model in depth, it's useful to understand the basic neuroscience behind how our mind and body work together.

The Motion is the Memory

We often talk about "muscle memory" in golf. Grooving your swing. Pitch shots or putts you've practiced so many times they're automatic. Repeatable motions you can trust under pressure.

But your muscles don't have memory. The proper term is "motor memory."

Memory lives in your brain—specifically in the neural circuits that produce the motion. Understanding where that memory resides, and how it works, changes how we should think about practice and play.

What Motor Memory Actually Is

When researchers use fMRI (functional magnetic resonance imaging) to watch what happens in the brain during motor learning, they've discovered that motor memories aren't stored as descriptions of movements. They're stored as the movements themselves—as patterns of neural activity that directly produce the action.

Motor memory resides in a network of brain regions including the basal ganglia, premotor cortex, cerebellum, and parts of the inferior parietal cortex.[14] But it's not stored there like a video file on a hard drive. The memory lives in the same circuits that produce the action—the motor cortex, basal ganglia, and spinal cord motor neurons.[15]

Think about that for a moment. The pattern that creates your golf swing is the memory of your golf swing. There's no separate file called "my driver swing" stored somewhere in your head. The memory is the executable program—the precise sequence of neural firing that produces the motion.

This is why the basal ganglia contribute to incremental learning of stimulus-response associations.[16] You're not learning about the swing. You're encoding the swing itself as a learned response pattern. The motion is the memory.

The Efficiency Paradox

Here's where it gets interesting. If you watched someone's brain activity while they learned a new golf skill—let's say a bunker shot—you'd see something counterintuitive.

In the beginning, when they're consciously thinking through every element of the technique, their brain lights up like a Christmas tree. High activity in the frontal and parietal lobes. Slow, clumsy execution = lots of cognitive effort.

As the golfer gets better at the bunker shot, brain activity actually decreases as the brain becomes more efficient.[17] The most skilled players show less neural activity during execution, not more.

We assume mastery means the brain is working harder. The opposite is true. Mastery means the brain is working smarter—using fewer resources to produce better and more consistent results.

Studies in young adults typically demonstrate an overall reduction in activity when learning progresses, indicating increased neural efficiency.[18]

From Conscious to Unconscious

What's actually happening during this efficiency shift? The brain is moving the skill from conscious control to automatic execution.

There is a smooth transition from the visual-cognitive to the motor loop, with a *switch* from anterior to posterior circuits, from declarative learning to optimization networks.[19]

In plain English: when you first learn a bunker shot, you're using the parts of your brain that handle conscious thought, attention, and problem-solving. You're thinking your way through it.

As skill develops, the work transfers to a different system entirely—the basal ganglia and cerebellum. These structures operate below the level of conscious awareness. They're specialists in automatic execution.

The basal ganglia don't think about the motion. They produce it. This system underlies procedural memory, which supports the learning and execution of motor and cognitive skills, especially those involving sequences.[20]

The motion runs automatically. Below awareness. That's why we don't need to worry that when we raise a fork there will be a seamless transfer of food to our open mouth.

What This Means When Practicing

If the motion is the memory, and the memory is encoded as a neural pattern that directly produces the movement, then what are you actually doing when you practice?

You're not practicing the shot. You can't. The shot is an outcome—where the ball goes, how it curves, whether it stops near the pin. Outcomes are affected by your motion, but they're not created by your intention. They're created by physics responding to the motion you produced.

You're practicing the motion. You're encoding—through repetition and refinement—the neural pattern that produces that motion.

Every swing is either reinforcing an existing pattern or creating a new one. The basal ganglia contribute to incremental learning of stimulus-response associations.[21] That's the mechanism. *Stimulus* (I need to hit this bunker shot), *response* (this motion), *association* (this is what I do in this situation).

Do it enough times with enough attention to the motion itself, and the pattern becomes automatic. The memory becomes reliable. The motion becomes uniquely yours.

Why the Distinction Matters

When you step up to a shot on the course and start thinking about the outcome—I need this to stop within six feet, I can't go left, this has to be perfect—you're engaging the wrong system.

You're activating the conscious, cognitive parts of your brain that were helpful during the learning phase but are terrible during execution. Implicit motor learning is governed by procedural memory and occurs below the level of awareness, while explicit motor learning involves conscious recollection.[22]

The motion you've practiced—the one encoded in your basal ganglia as an automatic motor program—doesn't need your conscious mind's help. In fact, conscious interference often makes it worse.

The shot you're trying to produce? That's not something you can control directly. You can only control the motion. The shot is what happens when clubface meets the ball.

This is the difference between trusting the memory you've built and trying to consciously manufacture an outcome in real-time.

The Motion Runs Itself

Motor memories are stored in circuits which mediate the behavioral motor pattern.[23] The pattern lives in the circuits that run it. When you've practiced a motion enough, when it's truly encoded as motor memory, it doesn't need conscious supervision.

All it needs is permission to run the sequence.

The key is to find your *switch* from analytical to intuition. From trying to control the shot to allowing the motion to play out. From effortful conscious control to efficient automatic execution. From brain activity lighting up to brain activity quieting down.

Incorporating Memory into Practice

It's much harder to stop thinking about mechanics (conscious control) when standing over a shot, than it is to find that mind state that allows your procedural memory to produce the motion. *You can't think your way into not thinking.*

Trying to force yourself to "stop analyzing" just creates another layer of conscious effort. Instead, you need to redirect your attention—give your conscious mind something to do that doesn't interfere with execution.

Some people can more easily tune out distractions than others. The Swing to Flow process offers a way to identify ways to train your mind to be better at this. The model discusses ways to integrate *mechanics*, *mindfulness*—the key to calming the mind—and *intuition* that allows your procedural memory to run the swing.

The motion is the memory. Practice the motion, play the memory.

I realize that's a lot, so feel free to take a break and let it sink in. When you're ready, we'll move to the first element of the model: mechanics.

Without solid mechanics, there is no golf. But here's what's interesting—even the way we define golf mechanics reveals how much we don't talk about the mental game.

Mechanics

Most golf instruction defines the swing purely in physical terms. After researching a wide spectrum of golf literature, here's what I found as the typical definition of golf mechanics:

The application of the body's movements required to perform an effective golf swing, integrating principles of physics, biomechanics, and motor control to optimize performance and consistency on the course.

Read that carefully. Notice what's missing?

Nearly every golf definition focuses on physical mechanics while ignoring the mind's role entirely. The word "application" frequently appears—perhaps as shorthand for mental involvement—but how do we apply? The vagueness is telling. We know the swing follows physical laws, which are clearly spelled out. They tell us to *apply* body movements in accordance with immutable laws, without explaining how.

This is the gap the Swing to Flow process seeks to address.

Here's the reality check: total mechanical perfection remains virtually unattainable. Even tour professionals miss shots. Consistent golf is only attainable when we train the physical elements of our swing to work with our intuitive mind as an equal partner.

When we struggle to achieve consistency in our swing, we instinctively search for mechanical tips because they promise to make things simple, because we believe these fixes are the application mentioned in the definitions.

But tips are not applications, they are movements of our body. We want complexity to be simple, but when we rely on quick fixes, complexity actually increases. We are left with a mind cluttered by a jumble of swing thoughts that lead to confusing mechanical spirals. All this noise disrupts the flow of natural movement and ignores an untapped superpower, our mind. The fixes are crowding out access to our pure swing.

This is why you feel frustrated despite knowing more about swing mechanics today than you did last year. We are accumulating technical knowledge but not acquiring mindfulness knowledge at the same rate. When we do something different or new and it works, we're inspired. That spark—which resides in only in our mind—acts as a catalyst that can transform mechanical knowledge into fluid, effective motion.

Inspiration is the process of being mentally stimulated to do or feel something creative. It's a mental construct that breathes life into mechanics when it stalls. It's the bridge between knowing what to do and actually being able to do it under pressure.

There is story after story about tour golfers who find themselves in a putting slump. Then someone hands them a new putter or suggests a grip change. Suddenly every putt goes in—at least for a while. Was that mechanical transformation or inspiration that temporarily activated a deeper mental process that was already there?

This is where the Swing to Flow process can be helpful. Swing mechanics form the foundation, but they're brought to life only when you become fully present, and ignite your intuitive mind.

When your body and mind work as one, your swing mechanics become an unconscious expression of your mind's intention, rather than a collection of positions or moves you're trying to remember.

This is the difference between mechanical golf and golf mechanics that incorporates intuition. It's what separates consistent players from those who struggle despite having good swings on the range.

Here is my definition of golf mechanics:

The integration of physical motions with mindful present-moment awareness to perform an effective and repeatable golf swing, combining principles of biomechanics and motor control, as well as intuition and flow states, to optimize both presence and performance on the course. [24]

Next up is the second pillar of the Swing to Flow process: mindfulness. We'll look at what mindfulness is and how to incorporate it into your game to increase performance and enjoyment.

Mindfulness

I become so involved in that particular moment... There are many putts or shots where I don't remember hitting the ball. —Tiger Woods [25]

If you study video footage of Tiger Woods from his early dominance through his remarkable 2019 Masters victory, one thing becomes unmistakably clear: he operates on a different mental plane than everyone else on the course. His face reflects a stoic, calm intensity, his demeanor is one of unshakable focus, and his comment about not remembering that he made a swing, reveals something profound: when Tiger is at his best, his analytical mind fades into the background, allowing his deeper intuitive intelligence to lead the swing. He has mastered mindfulness and plays most of his golf in the flow.

I believe mindfulness might be the greatest untapped opportunity in golf for recreational players.

Beyond Golf: A Universal Principle

Mindfulness extends far beyond golf. Shohei Ohtani, arguably baseball's greatest two-way player since Babe Ruth, has built his $700 million career on mental foundations.

Since high school, Ohtani has practiced visualization techniques, imagining game scenarios to strengthen neural pathways before he ever steps on the field. He used the Harada Method—a comprehensive goal-setting system—to map not just his baseball skills but his complete personal development. And he's been a dedicated practitioner of Tempu Methods, a form of Japanese yoga focused on mind-body integration, since his teenage years.[26]

His manager with the Angels noted that what impresses most isn't

Ohtani's physical talent, but "how he prepares his body, his mind, even sleep, to be the best." Different sport, same mental mastery. The tools change, but the principle remains: elite performers quiet their analytical minds and access something deeper.[27]

What Mindfulness Means for Golfers

Mindfulness is intentionally focusing attention on the present moment, while calmly acknowledging and accepting feelings, thoughts, and bodily sensations—without judgment.[28]

In the context of golf and the Swing to Flow process: mindfulness is what you develop through mental practice, while being fully present is how you perform when playing. When applied to golf, mindfulness means being unconditionally engaged in each moment, from the time you arrive at the course to sinking the final putt on the eighteenth green.[29]

It's the foundation upon which sustained peak performance is built. Unlike physical mechanics, which are limited by athletic ability, size, and strength, mindfulness unlocks a realm of possibilities with elastic boundaries that can be expanded through practice.

A Brief History of Mindfulness

Mindfulness can be traced back to South Asia between 2300 and 1500 BC, but it didn't spread to the Western world until the 19th century through colonialism and cultural exchange. In the 1970s, mindfulness was cleaved from its religious roots by psychologists and validated through extensive research, particularly regarding mental health, cognitive functioning, and overall well-being.[30,31]

This isn't just theory or philosophy. Mindfulness and meditation are backed by extensive neuroscience research.[32, 33]

Psychologists actively use it to help people perform under pressure. It is paying attention on purpose—staying in the here and now without getting pulled into thoughts about what happened or what might happen next.

The Power of Being in the Present Moment

Mindfulness is the discipline you cultivate. Present-moment awareness is how you apply it on the course.

Present-moment awareness in golf consists of two complementary modes—open and focused. Open awareness is expansive—it creates the mental space required to see the full picture, identifying trouble spots and multiple shot options. Focused attention is the opposite: it narrows to a single frame, filtering out distractions from past shots or future outcomes.

Mindfulness and Sports Psychology

Sports psychology is not new. It was introduced in Berlin in 1920, but didn't gain widespread acceptance until the 1970s. As competition intensified across sports, athletes began exploring mental performance training to gain an edge. Today's sports psychologists employ strategies ranging from goal setting and self-talk, to visualization, relaxation techniques, performance analysis, and team dynamics.[34, 35]

According to the U.S. Olympic Committee, 90% of Olympic athletes incorporate imagery work into their training and competition routines. Visualization is an active, constructive practice while mindfulness emphasizes present-moment awareness, the two approaches complement each other.[36]

Golf instruction has increasingly emphasized 'the mental game' as essential to consistent performance. *The Inner Game of Golf* by

Timothy Gallwey (1979) stands as one of the earliest guides. He emphasized the importance of mastering one's inner thoughts and emotions to improve play.[37]

Golf Mindfulness in Action

Think of what it takes to ride a bicycle—you need balance to stay upright, forward motion to keep moving, and the ability to steer and stop without overcorrecting.

In golf, mindfulness requires similar elements: presence to stay focused on each shot, continuity to move forward without dwelling on mistakes, and the ability to observe results without emotional interference.

The Architecture of the Moment

As our mindfulness develops, being fully present will become increasingly natural. It creates an inner tranquility that allows us to erase distractions, make better decisions, and keep emotions in check. This should be every golfer's starting point for improvement because it transforms how we experience the game at the most fundamental level.

Consider this: imagine a brief moment, then feel it vanish into the past. This happens non-stop throughout your round. Every moment arrives then departs, becoming sealed away in the vault of time past. It can't be replayed, and there's no good reason to dwell on it because another moment has already arrived. A fully present golfer embraces each moment—and only that moment—while playing.

Time moves in only one direction, but it leaves traces. Moments deposit things in memory that can be retrieved later. You have boundless mental energy to access your accumulated wisdom when needed. A calm, well-organized mind provides an advantage in this area.

Each Shot is an Offer

What if we framed each shot (moment) as an offer—an opportunity to respond to the current state of things on the course. The more fully present you are, the more often your response will be thoughtful and measured rather than emotionally reactive. Mindfulness helps your spontaneous reactions emerge from your intuitive mind and unlock flow states.

The next moment (shot) is about to arrive... Here it is... and you're alone again, faced with another offer. You accept the outcome of a poor shot and continue. You don't become overly excited after a great shot. Both responses—dwelling on failure or celebrating success—pull you away from the present moment where the next shot must be played.

The Trap of Wasted Moments

Wasting moments is far too easy. If you're looking at your scorecard on the fifteenth tee thinking you need to par out to break 90 or 80, you're wasting moments and energy that could actually help you get there. We have exactly the right number of moments needed before the final putt drops. How many moments? It's always ONE, and that moment is always NOW.

Managing Distractions

Distractions constantly arise from various sources—work concerns, family issues, or even song lyrics stuck in your head. These intrusive thoughts aren't who you are, but they are part of the human experience, and you can't always control when they arise.

Consider how dreams work. You wake from a vivid dream, your mind briefly acknowledges the content, and then—without effort—those dreams fade as you move into your day. You don't force them away; they simply dissolve. Distracting thoughts during your round can work the same way: acknowledge them, then let them fade without struggle.

As you develop stronger mindfulness, it becomes easier to acknowledge thoughts without judgment and more quickly return attention to the present.

The Physiology of Presence

When golf analysts speak about a player who's playing well, they often mention demeanor: "He looks really relaxed" or "she appears very comfortable." This relaxation is a natural result of presence—the absence of mental distractions. When the mind is quiet and focused, muscles don't receive tension signals. Uncoiled muscles are a direct result of ease, which opens the door to self-confidence.

Confidence vs. Fear

Self-confidence in golf is the belief in our ability to execute the shot at hand. It's recognizing that in this moment, you are the only person who can make the shot, and you possess everything required to do so. Self-confidence fosters self-trust—empowering traits that enrich natural abilities and serve as a protective shield against fear.

Fear is the enemy of presence. Facing a fast downhill putt, we sometimes make a weak stroke. "I was afraid it would get away from me," usually follows. Once fear creeps into our minds, it becomes incredibly difficult to eliminate because it pulls us into imagined future disasters. When we allow thoughts of fear to take root, they quickly multiply. The best defense against fear is cultivating a self-confidence that comes from being fully present and trusting our preparation.

Handling Adversity

There will be times when we lose our ability to stay in the present. One such situation might be when facing a challenging shot immediately following a poor one. The smart play is always to choose the shot that makes the next one as easy as possible. It's a tall order because after a poor shot, frustration emerges, and we sometimes revert to a "going through the motions" swing phase—we've lost our present-moment awareness.

When it comes to a golf shot, there's no second chance. The shot you just hit is in the past; the shot you're facing has a bright future. Which one do you want to prioritize in your mind? We can only hit one shot at a time, so keep your mind focused on that one.

The Zigzag Nature of Golf

Golf travels across acres of landscape, and this also presents opportunities for presence. If we mishit our drive into trees or a bunker with a high lip, we might experience heightened stress that affects our ability to stay in the present. Our spontaneous reaction when we stray from the intended path is to get back on track immediately.

But wanting to force our way back on track is at odds with golf's natural zigzag nature and the acceptance that presence requires. When a Formula 1 driver veers off track, they have no choice but to get back on it—all cars are on a one-way street. Golfers always have choices. Just look around.

When you find yourself out of position, accept what has happened and take the next few moments to explore other options. Some might not seem appealing, like hitting sideways out of a fairway bunker. I see players constantly hit into a bunker and immediately aim for the green on the next shot, and hit in the bunker beside the green. Don't compound an error.

Presence allows us to calmly play out an alternative shot in our mind:

imagine punching out of the bunker into the fairway with a great angle to the green. We're simply creating a new and better path forward—one that recognizes reality instead of fighting it.

This is the power of mindfulness in golf: it transforms obstacles into opportunities, fear into confidence, and scattered energy into focused action. Each moment becomes a fresh start, each shot a chance to practice the art of being fully present, fully engaged, and fully alive to the possibilities that unfold with each swing.

Understanding Mindfulness vs. Meditation

Let's clear up a common confusion: mindfulness and meditation are related but distinct practices.

Mindfulness is awareness of the present moment without judgment. You can practice it anywhere—doing laundry, walking to the next tee, or standing over a putt. It's about noticing what's happening right now and letting unrelated thoughts pass like train cars moving through a station. You observe without trying to change or fix anything. You're training your mind to eliminate distractions.

Meditation is structured mental training. It's a gym workout for the mind. You set aside time, find a quiet space, and use specific techniques—focusing on your breath, scanning your body, or repeating a phrase—to strengthen your attention. Meditation is active practice with a purpose: building the capability to be mindful when it counts.

Meditation appears passive from the outside but actually requires deliberate mental effort and conscious engagement. The activity in meditation is subtle but real—it's the difference between daydreaming (passive) and purposeful mental training (active). [38, 39]

Can you become fully present without meditation?

Some people can, but for most of us it's like trying to groove a reliable swing without practice—you might occasionally hit a pure shot, but you're not using the full toolkit. Homer Kelley, who wrote the encyclopedic *The Golfing Machine*, put it perfectly: "Are there any shortcuts? Indeed, and typical of shortcuts, they can easily turn out to be the longest route."[40]

Meditation trains your mind in a controlled environment so that when pressure hits on the course, presence becomes more readily accessible. Traditional meditation systems were designed as complete paths on their own, but combined with real-time mindfulness, they can foster sustainable inner peace.

Addressing Common Resistance to Meditation

Some golfers may dismiss meditation as too soft for them, or worry it conflicts with their beliefs.

Meditation isn't a religious belief—it's mental mechanics. You can meditate to build mindfulness without abandoning your beliefs or adopting new ones. Think of it this way: golfers spend hours on the range. Why wouldn't they spend time training their mind? Both are practice. Together they give you an edge.

Getting Started with Meditation

You don't need a guru to start. Pick up a book, download an app, or simply sit quietly for five minutes focusing on your breath. The barrier to entry is low. The payoff is substantial.

Meditation doesn't require sitting cross-legged in silence—there are practical forms that fit into daily life. Breath awareness, walking meditation, and body scans offer accessible entry points.

I practice both mindfulness and meditation daily, and modern technology has made this easier than ever. I use a smartphone app called *Insight Timer*,[41] which offers an extensive library of guided meditations. Combined with my Buddhist practice, these daily sessions sharpen my present-moment awareness.

Tai Chi: Meditation in Motion

An alternative to sitting meditation is Tai Chi, the traditional Chinese martial art that combines slow, flowing movements with deep breathing—often called meditation in motion. While popular among older adults, Tai Chi is suitable for people of all ages and fitness levels.

The practice emphasizes quality of movement over quantity, making it ideal for eliminating awkward movements in your golf swing. Numerous books, apps, and videos are available to help you explore whether it might be an option for you.[42]

Breath: The Foundation of Physical Presence

The connection between breath control and golf performance is easy to spot. Notice the difference between your breathing during a casual practice swing versus standing over a crucial putt. Controlled breathing can calm your heart rate before a crucial shot, help maintain tempo during your swing, and provide a reset mechanism between holes when emotions run high.

Simple techniques like taking three deep breaths before addressing the ball or using specific breathing patterns during your pre-shot routine can be transformative. When you are stressed you tend to speed up. Try to slow things down during those times. The faster you move, the harder your heart and brain work to keep up.

Bryson DeChambeau—sometimes known as the Mad Scientist—uses sensors that measure breaths per minute. He uses neurofeedback machine to train his brain to remain calm by controlling his breath.[43]

Breathing routines can be practiced anytime, anywhere. In *Breath: The New Science of a Lost Art* (2020), James Nestor posits that modern lifestyle, diet, and environmental factors have led to increased mouth breathing, which causes numerous health issues. He offers specific breathing exercises and emphasizes that changing how we breathe can provide measurable health benefits and boost athletic performance.[44]

I've adopted breathing exercises from his book, and they've improved my ability to control my breathing. It turns out we've dramatically underestimated the power of breath. We've been conditioned not to think about breathing because it's automatic—part of the autonomic nervous system. While technically true, our lungs are far more than just a system for processing oxygen into carbon dioxide.

Summary

Mindfulness in golf is not focused on improving your score—though it is a pleasant byproduct. It's about experiencing the game, with greater presence, clarity, and joy. Every round becomes an opportunity to practice these skills, every shot a chance to return to the present moment. The journey toward playing mindful golf is lifelong, but the benefits begin immediately:

- **Awareness**: Start by simply noticing when your mind wanders
- **Nonjudgment**: Progress to observing without criticism
- **Nonreactivity**: Develop your ability to maintain emotional equilibrium
- **Patience**: Cultivate your trust in the process

- **Letting Go**: Release attachment to outcomes

In doing so, you'll discover that golf becomes not just a game you play, but a practice that develops mental qualities serving you far beyond the eighteenth hole. This is the power of mindfulness—it can transform both your golf and your everyday life, one present moment at a time.

Mindfulness alone isn't enough. You can be fully present, aware of every detail, and still struggle if you can't trust what you've practiced. This is where the third pillar of the process comes in: intuition.

Intuition

Intuition (intuitive mind) is the ability to understand or know something instantly without conscious reasoning. It uses rapid subconscious pattern recognition and information processing, bypassing the need for conscious thought.[45]

When Lee Trevino was playing in the 1972 Open Championship on the Muirfield course in Scotland, he won largely because of his amazing putting performance. In the 2024 documentary, *Lee Trevino: An American Dream*, he said that he never even lined up most of his putts during that tournament. He just "saw the line" and made the stroke.[46]

Elite players have mastered swing mechanics as well as their ability to trust their intuition. The shot appears effortless because they've already mentally rehearsed it well before addressing the ball. At that level, execution becomes almost a formality—an inevitable outcome of present-moment awareness guided by intuition.

Neuroscience research has long validated the existence of two brain functions—analytical and intuitive—and their distinct roles in decision-making and performance. In a 2015 study, Geoffrey Schweizer, Alex Bertrams, and Philip Furley applied this dual-process framework to athletics, demonstrating that elite performers alternate between analytical and intuitive processing to meet the complex demands of competitive sport.[47]

The Analytical Mind

The left hemisphere of our brain excels at logical thinking, sequencing, and analytical processing. This translates to precise calculations and detailed observations. When you note that the wind is from behind, the distance to the flagstick is 153 yards, and you conclude that an

8-iron is the appropriate club; thank your analytical mind. This part of your brain is always on high alert and stands ready to prepare you for each shot; gathering and processing data needed for sound decision-making.

The Intuitive Mind

But golf requires more than math. Even with solid mechanics, the subtler aspects of the game—feel, tempo and touch—resist analytical breakdown. These elements aren't easily translated into concrete principles, making them difficult to understand through logic alone.

Our intuitive mind specializes in imagination, holistic perception, and pattern-based processing. When you sense a downhill putt will break slightly to the right, or feel that you need to take a little off your 9-iron for an approach shot, your intuitive mind is guiding you through patterns and feel that allow you to execute with confidence.

In golf, the analytical mind leads during course management decisions, pre-shot routines, as well as structured practice sessions, while the intuitive mind takes over when visualizing shots, reading greens, and adapting to unusual circumstances as needed. Both work together by integrating technical knowledge with feel and creativity.

You've now been introduced to all three pillars of the Swing to Flow process. Each is powerful on its own. But when all three are in sync—when solid technique meets present-moment awareness and joins complete trust—something extraordinary can take place. You enter a state of flow.

State of Flow

What if nothing could distract you? What if every swing felt effortless, automatic and joyful? That's being in flow—and it's accessible to you.

Flow isn't a mystical spell—it's a natural mental condition available to almost anyone. In golf, this state offers the ability to execute a sequence of multiple ideal shots, opening the door to significantly lower scores.

The Science Behind Flow

The father of flow research is Dr. Mihaly Csikszentmihalyi (1934-2021), a pioneering Hungarian-American psychologist. In his book, *Flow: The Psychology of Optimal Experience* (1990), he integrates a vast body of research on consciousness, personal psychology, and spirituality. He observed many ways a positive mental state can be controlled rather than left to chance.

Dr. Csikszentmihalyi writes:

I developed a theory of optimal experience based on the concept of flow—the state in which people are so involved in an activity that nothing else seems to matter; the experience itself is so enjoyable that people will do it even at great cost, for the sheer sake of doing it.[48]

He notes the phrase "even at great cost." Golf demands plenty of it—time, money, ego, and the emotional toll of a game that humbles everyone who plays it. Yet we keep coming back, for the sheer sake of doing it. That's the pull of golf in the flow.

Dr. Csikszentmihalyi continues:

Control over consciousness is not simply a cognitive skill. At least as much as intelligence, it requires the commitment of emotions and will. It is not enough to know how to do it; one must do it, consistently, in the same way as athletes or musicians who must keep practicing what they know in theory.[48]

Since his groundbreaking work, psychologists have continued studying flow states, developing measurement scales and conducting neuroscientific research using brain activity monitoring. Today, sports psychologists, educators, and workplace productivity experts apply flow principles across various situations.

Have You Been in the Flow?

Think of a time when you were so engrossed in work or a hobby that you lost track of time. You looked up and suddenly realized hours had passed. Dr. Csikszentmihalyi would say you changed the contents of your consciousness without even trying. How? Because there were no distractions, no threats—only order in your mind. Your attention was freely and fully invested in the present moment (also referred to as "in the zone").

When a person is able to organize his or her consciousness so as to experience flow as often as possible, the quality of life is inevitably going to improve... In flow we are in control of our psychic energy, and everything we do adds order to consciousness.—Dr. Csikszentmihalyi.[49]

I experience flow states while writing or working on projects around the house. I also enter flow states while playing golf, but extending flow beyond a handful of swings is challenging. We have all followed up a birdie with a bogey on the very next hole. This book is the result of my quest to access flow states more often and extend them for longer periods of time while playing.

Characteristics of Flow States

Through hundreds of interviews, Dr. Csikszentmihalyi identified commonalities that subjects reported when experiencing flow. They are: a loss of self-consciousness, a sense of discovery, creative feelings of being transported across time to a new reality, and higher levels of performance.[50]

Loss of Self-Consciousness

This phrase may be ominous, so clarification is needed. Loss of self-consciousness is not losing your sense of self or actual consciousness. Rather, it's only an absence of awareness of the "concept" of self. The more we focus on ourselves (being self-centered), the more resistant we are to flow. If our thoughts center entirely on self, growth is held back. Paradoxically, losing self-consciousness helps us develop our true self. The concept of letting go to get more is crucial for accessing flow states. Research shows that when people become completely engrossed in a task, actions become spontaneous—there's no separation between who they are and their actions. When they're no longer aware of themselves, things flow.[51]

Altered Perception of Time

Flow states ignore the clock: Hours and minutes are artificial constructs. During optimal experiences, time no longer passes in an orderly manner. The activity we're undertaking operates on its own timeline rendering clock-watching worthless. People in flow often report that time passes much faster (time flies when you're having fun).

Flow activities move at their own pace, marking the passage of events without regard to equal intervals. A flow state might be the closest we can come to experiencing time travel.

Control and Consciousness

We enjoy having control over situations. Golf is a self-contained activity, which leads us to view it as a pursuit of self-control. As a result, we expend vast amounts of mental energy trying to control our physical actions while playing. This approach has significant limitations.

Elevating our golf consciousness proves difficult because the force that adversely impacts our awareness is disorder—information that conflicts with our intentions. Dr. Csikszentmihalyi warns, "We are the prey of our thoughts," and they never stop trying to dominate every moment.[51]

Many golfers rely on swing thoughts, but there are significant downsides to trying to control mechanics with them. When addressing the ball, we can remember only one or two thoughts at best. A solid golf swing requires that dozens of things go right—focusing on just two of them actually inhibits the performance of our intuitive mind, which can manage thousands of things at once. Many of our thoughts stem from fear, and fear usually wins the battle. The result can be trying to steer the ball away from trouble, disrupting a natural swing path.

The most powerful control we possess isn't physical—it's intuition. Steven Yellin, a sports psychologist who works with professional golfers, emphasizes that while understanding swing mechanics is crucial, "It's the mental processes that enable players to execute fluid and powerful motions."[52] Our brain has enormous processing power; why constrain it to one or two swing thoughts?

Creating Conditions for Flow

To encourage flow states, it helps to establish clear objectives. A goal might be making a smooth motion (swing with tempo) that results in solid contact. However, that is broad and open to interpretation. Numeric goals provide more clarity—they're either achieved or not. Score is often the first goal: total strokes (more on that later). Every time we address the ball, we're working toward a goal; make this par putt or get safely out of the bunker. We have goals for each hole (par or birdie) and for the round (breaking 80 or 90). There might also be long-term objectives such as attaining a lower handicap.

Set goals and track them—they're essential triggers for flow states. Just remember: goals measure outcomes, not process.

Collecting Feedback

A golf swing offers immediate feedback, available within seconds of triggering it. Receiving and processing this feedback is important. Often, the initial signal we receive is the quality of contact. The more we play, the better we become at understanding our shot making. The goal remains constant—make solid contact—but nuances emerge when we try to understand what actually happened and why.

Feedback informs us about swing mechanics, chipping technique, driving accuracy, our putting stroke, to name a few. When structuring goals, identify the specific feedback signals to pay attention to—what you see, feel, and sense after each shot. Doing so will offer richer insights.

Summary

Developing skill in improving your mental game is a gradual process that requires patience. Rather than expecting dramatic changes all at once, focus on progressive improvement that builds confidence and competence over time.

Perhaps most importantly, learn to release your grip on self-consciousness and the desperate need to control every outcome. When you stop worrying about how you're performing or what others might think, you free yourself to become fully absorbed in the experience of playing golf. Trust your preparation and allow yourself to dissolve completely into the present moment. In this state of total immersion, you are setting the stage for flow states to appear.

Flow is the goal—complete immersion, effortless swings, scores that energize you. But flow sounds mysterious, like something that happens by chance. It's not. Flow emerges when specific conditions align, and those conditions can be deliberately created.

The Model in Action

A flow state can appear when all three elements of the Swing to Flow framework are working together. But frameworks don't lower scores. Practice does. Learning to use it does. Having a systematic way to evaluate your mental game during actual rounds does.

Let's continue to explore the performance model, this time adding everyday language we might use on the course—how the three elements **sound** when we are in a State of Flow.

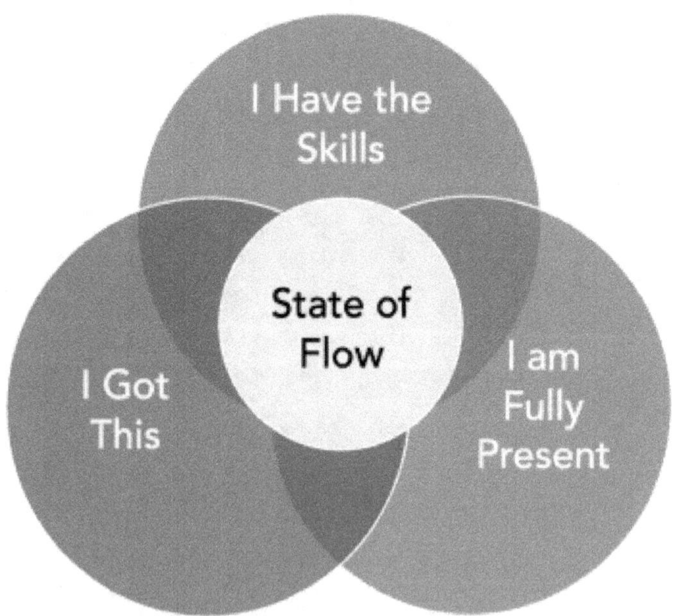

I HAVE THE SKILLS: This phrase brings to life the quiet confidence that comes from knowing you've practiced enough, that your swing is reliable, and you have the tools necessary for the shot at hand. It's the difference between hoping your swing works and knowing it will.

I AM FULLY PRESENT: This confirms you are all in, right here, right now—not replaying the last hole. It's the mental state where external distractions fade and only the current moment exists.

I GOT THIS: You are letting go of all mechanical thoughts, allowing your instincts guide the swing. You are moving from conscious control to unconscious competence, where feel takes precedence over thinking.

When all three of these elements are present, peak golf performance becomes attainable—not just your best golf, but golf that feels next-level and sustainable.

The power of this practical interpretation is that you can quickly assess where you stand during any round. Missing putts? Check your presence. Struggling with mechanics? Examine your skill confidence. Fighting your swing? Look at your trust level.

Measuring Golf Performance

The first thing most beginners do when they start playing golf is count strokes. Big mistake in my opinion. Here's the truth: strokes are meaningless when you first take up the game—perhaps even for the first couple of years. Every time you obsess over your score, you're focusing exclusively on mechanics and smothering the very things that will actually lower it: mindfulness and intuition.

If you are playing in a tournament, measuring your score jumps to the top of the list. But for the 90+ percent of golfers who never compete, obsession with score creates more pressure than progress. Lower scores are outcomes—the byproduct of process.

The vast majority of golfers never compete. Yet we obsess over stroke counts as if tournament play were our destiny, measuring our worth by a number that, for most of us, serves no functional purpose beyond bragging rights, and most certainly will not improve the playing experience.

Stroke count appeals to our need for simple measurement—like a grade on a test. But counting only strokes is fundamentally flawed. You can execute a perfect shot that catches an unlucky bounce and finds trouble, or hit a poor shot that gets a fortunate one and finds the green. When you track only outcomes, you *miss the real story of your performance.*

What is possibly the most important all-or-nothing action you can take immediately before you start your swing? Commitment.

Commitment

Most golf instruction treats commitment as a decide and trust exercise. But in the Swing to Flow process, commitment is the trigger for your intuitive mind. Commitment goes deeper than avoiding doubt—it's the pivot from preparation to execution, the moment mechanics, mindfulness, and intuition fuse into one.

I often hear golfers say to themselves while addressing the ball, "Commit to the shot." Or, after a poor shot, "I didn't commit."

Commitment is essential to skilled performance; full stop. But commitment is mental, not mechanical, which means it usually ends up at the bottom of a long list of things to remember while holding a club at address. We go through all the mechanical checks and motions in our pre-shot ritual, then at the last second before the swing we utter the words "commit to the shot", as if casting a spell.

Unless you're Harry Potter, that incantation is probably not going to be helpful.

What is Commitment?

A common definition: Committing to a shot is to fully accept club selection, target, and swing decision without doubt or hesitation during execution.

That is concise and accurate, but it doesn't help us learn *how* to commit. If we want to be more effective at committing to a shot, we must remember that body and mind are separate.

When we enjoy crisp tempo through the impact zone that leads to solid contact, and can do it four or five times out of ten, we are experiencing skilled, physical mechanics. This usually occurs on the range.

Commitment is needed on the course when we're facing our next shot; and that's all mental. Think about this for a moment. If you have mid-level swing skills and mentally commit to every shot on the course, your outcomes will probably equal your ball-striking range experience. But if you don't learn how to commit, even if you have above average swing skills on the range, you will probably perform below your shot-making skill level while playing.

The Mechanics / Mind Separation

Let's stay with the concept that mechanics is separate from the mind for a while longer. In your daily life when you are NOT practicing or playing, how often do you use your golf swing mechanics? It's not a trick question. Now, how often do you use your mind during the day? That's a useful observation.

Your mind operates 24/7; swing mechanics only matter for seconds at a time. Where should your real focus be when you need to commit to the swing?

How to Commit

The enemy of commitment is indecision driven by previous outcomes. When you stand over a shot and remember the last poor shot, you're activating the wrong part of your brain for what you're about to do.

Your swing lives in *procedural memory*—the same unconscious system that lets you tie your shoes without thinking. But when you're recalling past disasters or debating club selection mid-setup, you're using *declarative memory*—conscious recall. These two systems don't cooperate. They compete.

This is why indecision kills shots. Every moment spent second-guessing strengthens the analytical circuit and blocks access to the automatic one. *You can't think your way into a good swing, but you can think your way out of one.*

The Switch

Commitment isn't a moment. It's a strategy, a mode switch.

You gather information. You decide. Then switch—you move from planning to doing, from analyzing to trusting. The switch IS the commitment. It's the moment you stop wondering if you chose the right club and start swinging the club you chose.

Most golfers struggle to make this shift cleanly. They're still deciding while swinging. The body gets mixed signals: "Swing freely... but also be careful... but also commit... but what if..."

When you actually commit, your mind gets quiet. Not empty—quiet. You need to be fully present in that moment, not negotiating with your analytical mind. Your practice swing and course swing will feel the same because there's no mental interference between them. Time will seem to slow slightly. It's almost as if you're watching it happen in slow motion.

When you haven't committed, you know before you finish the backswing. There's tension. Hesitation. The voice inside you wonders what's going to happen while you're still in motion.

The Paradox of Commitment

Here's why full commitment is critical: A fully committed swing with the wrong club produces a better result than an uncommitted swing with the right one.

The ball responds to swing physics and contact quality, not to your doubts. A committed 7-iron that's one club short will fly straighter and more predictably than a tentative 6-iron where you're second-guessing mid-swing.

Understanding this can transform your experience. You don't need perfect information to commit. You need good-enough information, a clear decision, and the willingness to accept what happens next. In short, you're letting go (mindfulness).

The outcome isn't up to you. You can't control where the ball goes—only the quality of your commitment to the swing. Once you accept that, commitment becomes easier. And easier is something you can repeat.

Where Commitment Lives

You can't develop commitment on the course. The stakes are too high, the variables too many. Commitment must be trained on the range, but not by mindlessly hitting balls.

Pick a target—a specific one, not just "out there." Decide what shot you want to hit. Make that decision final. Then swing without interference and move on, regardless of outcome.

There is a drill I use. I set three balls on the range about two feet apart in a straight line away from my body. I swing at the first ball, then immediately move forward to the next and swing again. Then the third. Calmly, without rushing or thinking. It's effective because it offers no time to think between swings.

I knew an excellent instructor who wouldn't take any student who couldn't make solid contact on all three balls using this drill.

This is harder than it sounds because it requires mental discipline when there's no pressure, no score, nothing on the line. But that's the best place to train your brain to learn how to switch from analytical to execution mode. You're not just grooving your swing. You're grooving your ability to let go. To commit.

Commitment vs. Discipline

I think of commitment as strategy and discipline as tactics. Commitment is the decision—the *what* and *why*. You commit to a process, a practice philosophy, a way of approaching the game. Discipline is the *how*, repeatedly. It's doing the work when motivation fades—sticking with your routine on the 14th hole after three bad swings in a row. Commitment without discipline is just a good intention. Discipline without commitment is just going through motions.

Summary

Learning to commit to a golf shot is learning to commit, period. To make decisions. To act without perfect information. To trust yourself in the present moment. To accept outcomes without being paralyzed by them.

You can't fake it. But you can practice it. And once you accept that commitment isn't about mechanics at all, you stop trying to find it in your grip pressure or ball position. You find it in the shift from thinking to doing, from controlling to allowing.

Next comes the hardest part of the process: finding then flipping your switch—the method unique to you that activates your intuitive mind, allowing it to run the swing.

Flipping the Switch

In Swing to Flow terms: **Mechanics** provide the patterns. **Mindfulness** creates the conditions. **Intuition** executes the pattern. The practical challenge is learning to recognize when preparation is complete and execution should begin. That moment of transition—from "I Am Fully Present" to "I Got This"—is where most golfers struggle.

The switch from analytical to intuitive isn't a single technique—it's a skill you develop through deliberate practice. Different approaches work for different golfers. Experiment with these five methods to discover what helps you make that crucial transition—or create your own. If it works for you, it's right.

I am aware that I use the word "don't" repeatedly in the following methods. I do this intentionally, because stopping something is harder than starting something. Consider it an extra push.

1. Shift to an External Focus

Research on motor learning shows that focusing externally—on the target or the intended ball flight—produces better results than focusing internally on your body positions or swing mechanics.

There is a comprehensive 15-year study that essentially says: "an internal focus induces a conscious type of control, causing individuals to constrain their motor system by interfering with automatic control processes. In contrast, an external focus promotes a more automatic mode of control by utilizing unconscious, fast, and reflexive control processes.[53, 54]

After your practice swings, look at your target and see the shot. Not as a visualization exercise—just look and see where you want the ball to go. Let your eyes stay there as you make a practice swing. Your procedural memory knows how to send the ball toward what you're looking at.

Don't think about positions. Don't monitor your backswing. Just look at where you want the ball to go and trust the pattern you've practiced.

2. Use a Sensory Cue, Not a Mechanical Thought

Give yourself one feel or rhythm, not a body position or motion. Instead of "keep my left arm straight" or "turn my shoulders," use something like "smooth" or "low and slow" or even just breathe out as you start the downswing. For me it's a slight push of my left foot into the ground.

The cue triggers the pattern; it doesn't micromanage it. Your procedural memory understands rhythm and feel. It doesn't need instructions about elbow position.

3. Create a Clear Execution Signal

Your pre-shot routine should be about transitioning from planning phase to execution phase. The last thing you do before you swing should be the signal that says "the thinking is done, now I execute."

After you've aimed and settled, take one look at the target, return your eyes to the ball, and go. That last look is the signal. No gap. No extra thoughts. Look, return, swing.

I've had excellent results using this. The target isn't moving and your clubface is set—repeated checking only adds visual noise. This creates a clean break between analysis and execution.

This is why your pre-shot checklist is so important (See The Flow Score). It's a bridge. When you've worked through your checklist, that's your signal: analysis is done, intuition takes it from there.

4. Practice Without Conscious Monitoring

On the range, dedicate practice time to execution without evaluation. Not every swing needs to be analyzed.

Hit five balls in a row where you commit to swinging and watching the ball flight without any internal commentary about what you did right or wrong. You're training the ability to execute and observe without judging. Then hit ten in a row the same way. I dare you.

This is harder than it sounds. Your analytical mind wants to narrate every result. But learning to let the swing happen—and simply observe what happens—builds the trust that's essential on the course.

5. Trust the Misses

Your procedural memory won't be perfect every time. That's okay. The analytical mind jumps in when you don't trust the pattern to work. But learning to let imperfect swings run their course—without intervention—is part of building trust.

When you hit a less-than-ideal shot on the course, resist the urge to immediately diagnose and fix it. Just take note and move on. Save the analysis for practice. On the course, you're executing patterns, not building new ones.

Every time you accept a miss without panicking, you're strengthening the trust between your analytical and intuitive minds. You're teaching yourself that the pattern is reliable even when the result isn't perfect.

Recognizing Which Mind is in Control

How do you know which system is running?

Your analytical mind feels effortful. It narrates. It judges. It corrects mid-swing. When you're standing over a shot thinking "keep your left arm straight" or "turn your shoulders," that's analysis interfering with execution.

Your intuitive mind feels quiet, smooth, automatic. When you're looking at your target and your body just knows what to do—when the swing happens without conscious direction—that's intuition executing.

The difference is obvious once you learn to recognize it. During your next practice session, pay attention to how each swing feels internally. Not the result—the quality of attention during execution. When did you feel tight and controlled? When did you feel loose and flowing? That awareness is the foundation of deliberately making the switch. You're swinging freely.

Between Shots: Maintaining Presence

The time between shots is where rounds are won or lost mentally. Not because you need to "stay focused" every second, but because you need to stay present without needlessly burning mental energy.

You're standing on the tee or in the fairway and the group in front is still in range or on the green. Don't waste this time. Use it.

Create a Waiting Plan

Notice your environment. Wind direction and speed. Temperature. Cloud movement. The condition of the grass. You're gathering information without analyzing. This keeps your attention engaged without creating mental fatigue.

Stay physically connected to your mind. Feel your feet on the ground.

Notice your breathing. Do gentle stretches. Keep your body ready without rehearsing mechanics. Physical awareness anchors you in the present moment.

Use simple attention anchors. When your mind starts calculating scores or replaying shots, bring attention back to something immediate. Three conscious breaths. The feeling of the grip in your hand. The sound of stillness on an expansive golf course. These simple redirects prevent your analytical mind from spinning stories that create tension.

What to Avoid

Don't calculate scores, pace, or the number of holes remaining. Don't replay past shots. Don't build frustration narratives about slow players ahead of you.

All of these pull you out of the present moment and into either the past or the future. Neither helps you execute the next shot.

The Common Thread

Don't try to empty your mind or force yourself not to think. That creates tension. Instead, direct your attention somewhere that supports automatic execution rather than disrupts it.

Your procedural memory doesn't need help—it just needs permission to run.

The integration of Swing to Flow is a continuous practice. Some days the switch from analysis to execution feels effortless. Other days you'll catch yourself thinking mechanically mid-swing. That's normal. That's golf.

The goal is recognizing which mind is in control and having tools to make the transition when you need to. Over time, that transition becomes easier, smoother, more reliable.

We've covered a lot of ground. Everything so far has been about the mental approach to golf in harmony with mechanics—how to think, how to prepare, how to switch from analysis to intuition. But here's a question worth asking: you track every stroke on your scorecard, so why aren't you tracking what's happening in your mind between those strokes? The Flow Score gives you a way to do exactly that.

The Flow Score

Earlier, I emphasized the importance of not judging your shots, but now I'm going offer you a method for calculating your Flow performance. This might seem like a contradiction, but they are two very different things. Judging a shot is an emotional reaction to outcome: "That was terrible. What's wrong with me?" I just watched the Pebble Beach Pro-Am (Feb 2026). Sepp Straka, an elite ball striker, hit an approach shot into the rough 20 yards right of the green. He turned to his caddie and said, "I'm terrible at golf." Everything is relative. Emotional episodes can pull you out of the present and impact your next shot.

Other systems track mental game execution. The Flow Score tracks something different—integration. It measures whether mechanics, mindfulness, and intuition are working together when you swing. It asks a different question entirely: "Were all three elements present when I hit that shot?" It's not judgment—it's observation. Judging is reactive. Observing is reflective. Observing with data gives you the truth.

If we never evaluate we won't understand, making improvement nearly impossible. The goal is to separate evaluation from emotion, and to do it after the fact as useful data—not in a moment of self-criticism.

The concept of a Flow Score begins with a simple tool borrowed from professionals who perform under pressure in high-stakes jobs: the checklist.

The Power of Checklists

Airline pilots. They use checklists even after hundreds of successful flights because checklists reduce errors and create consistency under pressure.

In golf, checklists can serve the identical function. They establish a routine, and when you complete the checklist, it signals your intuitive mind that everything is ready for it to take control of the swing.

By following this routine consistently, you can create an objective standard for measuring your mental game.

Developing a Checklist

The most effective pre-shot checklists contain three to five short, actionable phrases that include mechanical fundamentals and intuitive elements. They're not random items—they are mental switch keys as well as things you do with your body. When these items are checked off, the shot has a very high probability of succeeding. Conversely, when even one element is missing, you'll likely produce a less than optimal swing motion.

Go back to the exercise you did in the Swing to Flow Process chapter. You made lists of the things you practice in two categories: mechanics and mental. Review your choices closely. You will probably want to update it given all you have read since. Resist the temptation to list as many things as you can think of. Challenge yourself to prioritize only the essential elements critical to your game.

Now, think about your most recent best shots. What was your mental state before the shot? What physical sensations did you notice during the motion? What was your preparation process? What do you see in your mind's eye when you recall them? These elements provide the raw material necessary to create your checklist.

By including both mechanical fundamentals and mental preparation elements, you create a bridge between technical knowledge and instinctive feel. Each item must be specific enough that you can definitively assess whether you completed it after the shot. Vague concepts like "stay relaxed" don't work because they're impossible to accurately measure. It would be better to use "arms and shoulders at ease" or an image of your target.

Sequence your checklist items in a logical order. This becomes your dress rehearsal. Keep each phrase short and actionable, using language that resonates with your personal way of thinking about golf. I sometimes close my eyes when I am going through my checklist as a way to block distractions. These personal touches matter—the checklist must feel like it belongs only to you.

Take your checklist to the range and methodically work through it, mentally checking off each item. Bring each element into conscious awareness as you prepare to make the shot. Once you have run through the checklist, execute the swing. After the shot, pause and honestly assess whether you fully carried out each element.

Airline pilots are mostly checking off mechanical elements: flaps positioned, fuel shutoff valve on, flight controls working, etc. Golfers have some mechanical checks related to grip, stance, alignment, etc. but the intuitive elements are hard to define and even harder to evaluate. That's why they are the most valuable.

The first few sessions will be the most important. It's classic trial and error. Drop elements that you can't evaluate cleanly and expect your checklist to evolve over time. What works on the range might not be as effective when playing. That's fine, adjust it. Updating the checklist is a good sign you are improving the process. Just guard against making spur of the moment changes. It will take some time to settle on a reliable list.

Flow Score by Shot

Once you've established your pre-shot checklist, convert each item to a yes/no question to be used for post-shot assessment.

My checklist below—at the time of writing this revised and expanded edition—has four items, two mechanical and two mental. Before each shot, I mentally run through the checklist, *before* I flip the Switch to intuitive mode. After the shot I take 15 seconds and determine whether I fully executed each item. If I did, I mentally note a "1" for yes. If I didn't fully execute any item, I note it as "0" for no.

In my post-shot assessment example below, Visualization and Core 4 (see The Core 4 chapter) were solid (1 for each). But I didn't fully commit to the shot, which usually means my tempo suffered, and it did (0 for each). Simple addition arrives at a Flow Score of 2 out of a possible 4; or 50% for that shot.

It's impractical to write down a Flow Score for every shot while playing, so I keep a running total in my head until I complete the hole. Your evaluation doesn't have to be perfect, and over time you will just do it out of habit.

FLOW SCORE BY SHOT

PRE-SHOT CHECKLIST	POST-SHOT ASSESSMENT		
Visualize the shot in detail	Did I visualize the shot?	Yes	1
The Core 4 Grip, posture, ball position & alignment	Did I lock in the Core 4?	Yes	1
Commit fully to the shot	Did I fully commit to the shot?	No	0
Tempo Slow backswing, pause at the top	Did I swing with tempo?	No	0

Mental Score for this Shot

2

Key Benefit of Using the Flow Score by Shot

Have you ever been playing poorly, then on the 15th hole something clicked in your mind and after a few seconds you realized you weren't doing that in your set-up or swing? Of course you have. We all have.

By using the Flow Score system on each shot, you will more quickly gain valuable insights that you can use on the very next shot, instead of wondering what went wrong and repeating it hole after hole.

Flow Score by Hole

After each hole, I follow this simple process. If I played a hole in 4 shots but only 3 of those shots satisfied ALL checklist items, I record "3" as my Flow Score for that hole. If only 2 shots achieved ALL items, record "2." I record these scores on the Flow Scorecard that I use instead of the course provided scorecard (more on that later). A hole's Flow Score can never exceed the stroke total, but it can be zero.

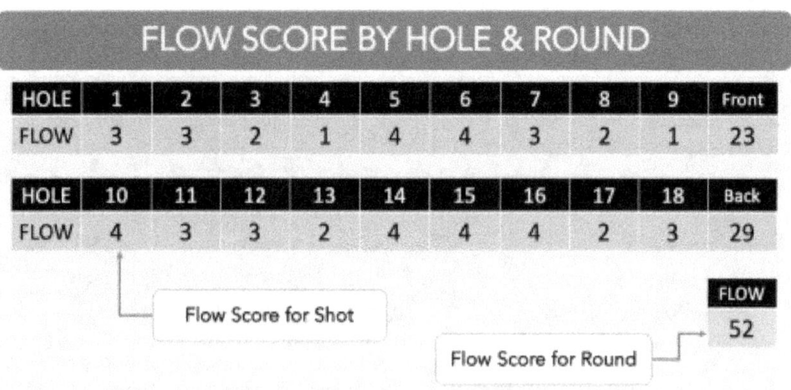

FLOW SCORE BY HOLE & ROUND									
HOLE	1	2	3	4	5	6	7	8	9	Front
FLOW	3	3	2	1	4	4	3	2	1	23
HOLE	10	11	12	13	14	15	16	17	18	Back
FLOW	4	3	3	2	4	4	4	2	3	29

Calculate Flow Score by Round

After the round, add up all hole Flow scores and divide that by the total number of strokes. For example, if you shot an 84 and your Flow score was 52, your Flow Index is 62%.

What you're measuring is simple: on what percentage of your shots did mechanics, mindfulness, and intuition work together? In the example, 52 out of 84 strokes = 62%.

This all-or-nothing system might feel limiting—after all, the intuitive mind doesn't operate in simple yes/no terms—but this limitation is its strength. It eliminates the gray areas where we might rationalize poor execution.

You can now measure something that's been invisible your entire golfing life: the quality of your mental game during play. Score it. Track it. Put it on your card right next to stroke count. No more vague feelings about whether you were fully present in the moment or allowed your intuitive mind to make the swing. You now have quantifiable data you can analyze.

We have always had the 18-hole stroke total. Now we have the Flow Index that, paired with your score, reveals new patterns and insights that can unlock real progress.

The Flow Index

The Flow Index offers something rare in golf: a performance measure that's 100% under your control. Bad bounces happen. Putts lip out. Greens get bumpy in the afternoon. Your score reflects all of that—skill, luck and the conditions.

The Flow Index reflects how consistently you accessed the integrated state where mechanics, mindfulness, and intuition worked together. Over time, pairing it with your score reveals patterns that strokes alone cannot.

Of course the instinct is to chase a Flow Index of 100%. That would be nice, but this falls into the same trap related to score. We want par or better on every hole, every time.

Flow Index to Score Patterns

Always pair your score with your Flow Index. By reflecting on them together you will get more data points and more insight into what to focus on.

High Flow Index and Good Score

Your stroke score was in line or perhaps below your handicap and your Flow Index was 75% or more. This is an everything aligned round—mechanics, mindfulness, and intuition working together to produce solid mechanics. This is validation. You accessed flow and it produced. This is the standard you're chasing.

High Flow Index but Poor Score

In this round you achieved solid integration on most shots, but the score didn't show it. Maybe the course was unusually brutal, conditions were tough, or you got bad bounces and your putts burned the edge of the cup over and over. Your Flow Index was still 75%—you succeeded at what matters. You controlled what you could control. Try to use this round to build confidence because this represents progress.

Low Flow Index with Good Score

This pattern is a false friend. You got lucky. You scrambled, ground it out, scored well—but you weren't actually accessing flow. Traditional scoring says you succeeded, so you might think you're trending up. The Flow Index below 60% reveals the truth: you can't rely on this. Red flag. You might regress unless you improve integration.

Low Flow Index and Poor Score

This is a learning opportunity. Neither process (below 60%) nor score (well above your handicap) were satisfactory. But here's the key: you know where to focus. You don't need to rebuild your swing or buy new clubs. You need to work on integration—getting mechanics, mindfulness, and intuition working together. Consider taking a swing lesson if these outcomes continue.

Score and Flow Index reveal patterns, but they're summaries. Each of your shots contains data that can expose exactly where your game is strong and where it breaks down. The Flow Scorecard captures over 20 additional data points per round—traditional stats like greens in regulation and putts, alongside Flow scores by shot and hole—giving you a more complete view of how you played and where to focus your practice.

The Flow Scorecard

Golf is a game of misses. Even the best players in the world are simply managing their mistakes far better than the rest of us. Ben Hogan said golfers should be satisfied with hitting just a few shots per round that feel absolutely perfect.

Hogan was right. Perfection is rare. Aspiring to achieve it is a fool's errand—like the apprentice sent to fetch a left-handed screwdriver.

So what separates those who improve from those who stay stuck? Data. Not emotion, not hope—objective information about what actually happens during your rounds. Before a shot, we think. After a shot, we feel. We calculate yardage, choose a club—then we swing and immediately react with joy or frustration. What gets lost is objective analysis. What actually happened? Why?

By building a pre-shot checklist and tracking Flow Scores by shot, hole and round, then calculating a Flow Index will produce valuable insights.

But there is so much more that can be tracked, so many more ways to help us understand what is taking place in our game and getting a better handle on what to work on to improve faster.

Data is King

Matt Fitzpatrick, a PGA player from England, is arguably the king of data on the tour. He is obsessed with numbers and believes it has been a major key to his success. He tracks dozens of data points in his yardage book real time while playing.[55]

He says:

I record the outcome of every shot in these books. I can show you 7,000 shots... It sounds a little over the top, but logging the numbers and reviewing them reveals an honest assessment of my game. Learning you miss to the right more often than left might influence your aim. Stats don't lie. (See Appendix for an image of his book)

I'm not suggesting everyone be like Matt. That's not reasonable and most players don't use yardage books. But all golfers who want to improve use a scorecard. What if you could bring Matt's analytical power to your scorecard?

Beyond the Score

You shot 90, or even an 81. What does that tell you? Almost nothing. Your score alone can't tell you why you shot what you shot or what you should work on. Even more critically, it ignores your mental state entirely—the invisible part of your game that often determines success or failure.

Did you spray drives left or consistently miss right? When you missed greens, were they all short, suggesting club selection problems? How well did you get it up and down? Was your putting sharp? Was it mechanics or mental? Without these answers, improvement becomes guesswork.

I developed the Flow Scorecard for myself to end the guessing. It captures the details that matter: fairway misses by direction, green misses by location, putting patterns, scrambling success, birdie conversion rates—and critically, all your Flow data, by shot, hole, round and of course the Flow Index.

The Flow Scorecard is a simple, free Excel file that you can **download** from **swingtoflow.com/downloads**. Type in two data points: the course name and the par for each hole and you're ready to play Flow golf. For those who like to capture all the details, you can include handicap by hole, tees, yardage, rating, slope, even pin location (all optional). Save it, print it and you're ready to play.

The example shows what a finished Flow Scorecard looks like at the end of a round.

The King Course - Arrowhead Date 11/15/25

Tees: White   Yds: 6,014   Rat: 69.3   Slope: 120   Pin: 3

HCP	7	17	9	15	5	1	11	3	13	
Front	1	2	3	4	5	6	7	8	9	Out
Par	4	5	3	4	4	5	3	4	4	36
Score	4	5	4	4	4	5	3	3	5	37
Fairway	1	1		1	R	1		1	L	5
Green	1	1	R	1	1	R	R	1	1	6
Putts	2	2	2	2	2	1	1	1	3	16
FLOW	4	5	3	4	3	4	2	3	3	31

HCP	8	12	14	2	6	16	18	4	10		
Back	10	11	12	13	14	15	16	17	18	In	Total
Par	4	3	5	4	4	3	4	4	5	36	72
Score	5	4	6	4	4	4	4	4	4	39	76
Fairway	1		R	L	1		R	1	1	4	9
Green	R	RT	ST	S	1	RT	1	1	1	4	10
Putts	2	2	2	1	2	2	2	2	1	16	32
FLOW	3	3	2	2	3	2	4	3	4	26	57

Birdies	2	1 Putts	5	Driving Accuracy	64%
Pars	10	3 Putts	1	GIR	56%
Bogeys	6	Putts +/-	-4	Fairway/GIR	78%
D Bogeys +	0			Birdie Conversion	20%
				Scrambling	38%
Flow Scorecard				FLOW Index	75%

How to Record Your Round

While playing, use this simple shorthand to mark how you played each hole. It only takes seconds to mark:

- **Strokes:** Note as you would normally
- **Hit it?** Mark "1" for fairways or greens
- **Missed it?** Note the direction: L, R, S, O
- **In trouble?** Add T for traps, LT, RT, ST, OT
- **Special cases:** LU (layup), OB (out of bounds), H (hazard)
- **Putts:** Note as you would normally
- **Flow Score:** Record your assessment as outlined in the Flow Score section
- **Flow Index:** Complete using the Flow Index section

Stroke and Flow Scoring (8 Data Points)

The top section capture strokes, of course, but also valuable information as explained above.

Score and Putting Summary (7 Data Points)

The left and middle columns in the lower section of the card sum up birdies, pars, bogeys, and double bogeys +. The middle section is where you record the number of one-putts, three-putts and putts +/- the standard 36.

Key Performance Indicators (6 Data Points)

The right side of the lower section shows percentage metrics:

- **Driving Accuracy**: Fairways hit ÷ driving holes: 9 fairways ÷ 14 holes = 64%
- **GIR Percentage**: Greens hit ÷ total holes: 10 greens ÷ 18 holes = 56%
- **Fairway/GIR Conversion**: Greens hit from fairways ÷ fairways hit: 7 greens ÷ 9 fairways = 78%
- **Birdie Conversion**: Birdies ÷ greens in regulation: 2 birdies ÷ 10 GIRs = 20%

80

- **Scrambling**: Successful up-and-downs ÷ missed greens: 3 saves ÷ 8 tries = 38%
- **Flow Index**: Total mental score ÷ total strokes: 57 ÷ 76 = 75%

Thirteen data points that, when analyzed, will reveal where strokes are gained or lost, which parts of your game hold up under pressure, and what deserves your practice time. Instead of having a sense of "playing well" or "struggling" you get a true picture of your performance.

If you're comfortable working with spreadsheets, the downloaded Excel Flow Scorecard file has a second tab with built-in formulas and color coding options, that offers an at a glance visual of the round making it easier to spot patterns.

Tee: White   Yds: 6,014   Rating: 69.3   Slope: 120   Pin: 3   Date

HCP	7	17	9	15	5	1	11	3	13		8	12	14	2	6	16	18	4	10		11/15/25
Hole	1	2	3	4	5	6	7	8	9	Out	10	11	12	13	14	15	16	17	18	In	Total
Par	4	5	3	4	4	5	3	4	4	36	4	3	5	4	4	3	4	4	5	36	72
Score	4	5	4	4	4	5	3	3	5	37	5	4	6	4	4	4	4	4	4	39	76
Fairway	1	1		1	R	1		1	L	5/7	1		R	L	1		R	1	1	4/7	9/14
Green	1	1	R	1	1	R	R	1	1	6/9	R	RT	ST	S	1	RT	1	1	1	4/9	10/18
Putts	2	2	2	2	2	1	1	1	3	16	2	2	2	1	2	2	2	2	1	16	32
FLOW	4	5	3	4	3	4	2	3	3	31	3	3	2	2	3	2	3	4	4	26	57

Fairways Hit	Birdies 2	1 Putts 5	Driving Accuracy 64%
GIR	Pars 10	3 Putts 1	GIR 56%
Up and Down	Bogeys 6	Putts +/- -4	Fairway/Green Conversion 78%
	Double Bogeys + 0		Birdie Conversion 20%
			Scrambling 38%
			Flow Index 75%

1 = Hit Fairway or Green   OB = Out of Bounds   H = Hazard   LU = Layup
L = Missed Left   R = Missed Right   S = Missed Short   O = Missed Over
LT = Missed Left Trap   RT = Missed Right Trap   ST = Missed Short Trap   OT = Missed Over Trap

    Flow Analytics Spreadsheet

The Story of Your Round

Pretend the Flow Analytics Spreadsheet above represents one of your rounds. Here's where it gets interesting. Let's see how patterns emerge that might otherwise remain hidden.

Flow Index: 76%

Three-quarters of your shots met all the complete Post-Checklist requirements. This strong mental performance provided the foundation for solid scoring. When mechanics and mind align at this level, lower scores tend to follow. Track this index over time along with your score.

Occasionally I will play a practice round and focus solely on my Flow Index.

Driving Accuracy: 64%

You hit 64% of fairways and 56% of **GIR**. More revealing: those 9 fairway hits produced 7 greens in regulation—a **78% conversion rate**. The pattern is clear: accurate drives don't just avoid trouble; they manufacture scoring opportunities. Miss the fairway, and reaching the green becomes harder. Of course great drives in the fairway don't automatically turn into a GIR.

Birdie Conversion: 20%

You hit 10 greens in regulation, creating 10 birdie chances. Only 2 were converted. That 20% birdie conversion rate represents golf's eternal frustration—solid approach shots don't guarantee birdies.

Our minds fixate on these missed opportunities while dismissing the positive overall performance. This is where your non-judgmental mindset becomes crucial: acknowledge good execution regardless of outcome, then get to work on the shortfall.

Putting: -4

Taking 32 putts—4 under the 36-putt regulation—with five one-putts and only one three-putt indicates good, but not great performance on the greens. With a better putting performance this round might have approached a personal best. Masters champion Hideki Matsuyama is known for his relentless putting practice—often spending hours on the practice green before and after rounds. You don't need to match a tour pro's schedule. But ask yourself: how much time do you spend on the range with your full swing, and how much on the practice green?

Scrambling: 38%

Converting 3 of 8 up-and-down attempts (38%) exposes a short game weakness that needs to be addressed. Additional analysis is needed: Did you fail to get it up-and-down because your chipping or sand play was poor, or because your putting wasn't sharp? Scrambling requires both a good chip and a good putt.

Consistent Misses

The data also reveals a concerning pattern: you're leaving yourself difficult recovery situations by consistently missing greens in the same location. Six out of 8 approach shots missed the green to the right and 3 of them landed in traps. All 3 trap misses resulted in zero successful up-and-downs. This highlights two things: you frequently miss right, and bunker technique needs practice.

The Par 3 Problem

You hit 10 greens with irons—but only one came on a par 3. Every par 3 miss went right. Not sometimes. Every single one. This might be due to some underlying issue that should not be overlooked. Without this data, that pattern probably gets lost in the emotion.

The Big Picture

Zero double bogeys means mistakes were contained. In golf, avoiding catastrophe often proves more valuable than chasing perfection. This round demonstrated mature course management—balancing aggression with discipline to keep a good round from unraveling.

This round was also strong in mental execution and fairway accuracy, while bunker play, chipping, putting, and iron accuracy are opportunities for improvement.

This is how data-driven progress works. Track the patterns. Practice with intention. Play with intelligence. That's your path from guessing to knowing.

You now have the Swing to Flow framework, the measurement tools and a robust system to collect and analyze your data. Next: practice that actually works. Not mindless ball-beating, but Intentional Practice—a systematic approach built on two distinct phases that mirror how you play on the course.

Intentional Practice

The range *lies* to you. Repetition every 10-15 seconds, identical setup conditions, zero consequences. The course tells the *truth*: extended time between shots, complete reassembly for each swing, no second chances, and every shot is different.

Golf is a sport full of paradoxes, and here's another one: the harder we try to control our swing, the more we interfere with our natural ability. Trying to force improvement, especially through rudderless repetition, creates confusion in our mind that can follow us to the course.

When you tell another golfer you're going to practice, it conjures up images of hitting balls on the range—which is what practice consists of for many golfers. But hitting balls isn't golf—it's boring and usually pointless. After a dozen or so shots your mind wanders but your body continues until the bucket is empty: "There, I've practiced."

Practice is a necessary component of improvement and ultimately enjoyment of the game, but it's time to move beyond the drudgery of range time.

What Is Intentional Practice?

Intentional practice is bringing your complete game—mechanics, mindfulness, and intuition—to every practice session, mirroring the approach you use on the course.

This mental commitment creates an equilibrium between play and practice, acknowledging the symbiotic relationship between the two elements and allowing them to strengthen each other.

Practice has two objectives:

- Continue simplifying mechanics so your intuitive mind can access them more easily during play
- Practice with focused attention on specific issues surfaced from your Flow Scorecard data.

Course play is where you *perform*—leveraging mechanics through mindfulness and intuition. Practice is where you *prepare*.

Two Modes of Practice

Swing to Flow creates this integration through two distinct modes: swing mode and target mode.

Swing Mode

When we start a range session, we're in swing mode. Where the ball goes is not important because the focus is on tempo and ball contact. We take note when we make flush contact and when we don't.

Here's where you can gather useful data. Pure strike or not—it's binary. After several swings, do a mental calculation to arrive at a ratio of pure shots to impure ones. Was it 3 out of 5? This simple metric reveals your current strike quality and, over time, tracks improvement in golf's most fundamental skill.

This is also where you work on mechanical aspects revealed by analyzing data from the Flow Scorecard. Perhaps you're smoothing out your transition, or working on the Core 4. In swing mode, you can give these elements attention without the pressure of outcome.

Target Mode

After several shots in swing mode, you begin to get more serious about direction. This signals you've shifted your focus to target mode. Suddenly where the ball goes is everything.

In target mode, you are modeling course play. Pick a specific target. Go through your full pre-shot routine including the checklist. Commit to the shot. Execute with trust. Then evaluate the result and move on, just as you would on the course.

This is where you work on strategic, decision-making issues. Maybe you need to practice committing to club selection, or trusting your alignment, or staying present through the shot. You might move to the practice bunker if you need to gain more confidence with sand play.

Mode Integration

Start combining swing mode and target mode in all your practice sessions going forward. Alternate between them intentionally. Spend time in swing mode working on mechanical simplification and contact quality. Then shift to target mode and put those mechanics into play with full commitment to a target.

You use your analytical mind to prepare for the shot, then allow your feel-based intuitive mind to take over and execute the swing.

This is how practice becomes purposeful rather than mindless. This is how the range stops lying to you.

Applying the Framework

The drills you choose matter less than how you approach them. Whether you're working with alignment sticks or distance control with wedges, apply the two-mode framework: use swing mode to isolate mechanics, then shift to target mode to integrate those mechanics with commitment and feel.

The specifics of your practice routine should be tailored to your individual needs. Work with a certified instructor who can identify weaknesses and design drills that can strengthen them.

The Play-Practice Partnership

When practice mirrors play, they strengthen each other. Course play reveals what needs work—your Flow Scorecard captures this data. Intentional practice focuses attention on those specific issues while continuing the ongoing effort to simplify your mechanics. When you return to the course with sharpened skills and refined mechanics, you'll gather new data to guide your next practice session.

The Fix Myth

We hear it constantly: "I need to fix that." After a range session: "I fixed it, I'm good." Here's the reality—there is no fix in golf, only adjustments. Golf doesn't have a destination where everything finally works and stays working. Your swing evolves. Conditions change. What worked last month needs tweaking this month. The sooner you replace the fix mentality with an adjustment mentality, the less frustration you'll carry and the more progress you'll make.

New Player? Start at the Hole, Not the Tee

Most new players start on the range with a driver, swinging away. I get the appeal—who doesn't want to crush it? But that's not learning golf, and it might be the worst possible starting point.

Getting Started

The journey takes patience, but less time than you think if you build the foundation correctly. Every hour invested in the right sequence creates skills that compound. This approach gives new players a manageable on-ramp to the game.

If you're exploring golf to see if it's for you, look for tutorial videos from certified PGA instructors that explain putting and chipping fundamentals. Focus on instructors who teach beginners, not the ones coaching tour players.

Get a putter and a pitching wedge—used clubs from a secondhand shop work fine, or borrow from a friend who's upgraded their set. Chances are they have older clubs gathering dust in the garage.

Locate a practice facility with a chipping and putting green. Avoid the range at this stage. Jumping into full swing mode will likely discourage you. If you didn't know how to swim but wanted to learn, would you climb to the top of the diving board and jump into the deep end?

If you start on the range and hit shots that get off the ground and go forward, you may think, "I'm a natural." Perhaps. Either way, the range doesn't offer the full scope of skills needed to play golf. Start with putting and chipping.

Learn the Short Game First

Once you've watched instructional videos or had someone teach you the fundamentals, you're ready. Drive to the practice facility.

Start with Your Putter

Begin with what will be your most important club. You'll use it more than any other, so build a relationship with it first.

Spend your initial time on the putting green. Find your grip, your stance, your stroke. Create a repeatable setup process. Learn to roll the ball smoothly. Read slopes. Work on those four-footers until they feel routine rather than nerve-wracking. You'll know you're ready to move on when you can stand over a putt and feel some level of confidence.

Take your time here. There's no deadline. When putting starts to feel natural, you're ready for the next step.

Add Your Wedge

Step off the green and pick up your second most important club: your wedge. Start chipping from various short distances toward targets on the green. Your body gets involved now—legs and hips participate in the motion. Tempo begins to take shape. Learn to make crisp contact, clipping the ball cleanly off the turf. Soon you'll feel the difference between a good chip and a thin or heavy one.

When chipping feels comfortable, combine the two skills. Chip to a target, then putt out. This becomes your rhythm: chip, putt, repeat. You're not just practicing shots anymore—you're learning how to score. No pressure, no scorecard, just the simple pleasure of getting the ball in the hole.

Stay here as long as it feels productive. This foundation is critical. Some players spend a few weeks, others longer. You'll know when you're ready to move ahead—when the short game feels comfortable and you're curious about what comes next.

The Range

Until now, you've practiced in a controlled environment—just you, the ball, and a clear target. You've learned what it takes to get the ball in the hole.

Now you need more clubs, but not many. Get a short iron (8 or 9 iron), a mid-iron (6 or 7 iron), a hybrid (4 or 5 hybrid), and a driver.

Watch tutorial videos designed for beginners, from certified instructors. Or tap that friend again for tips. If they'll accompany you to the range, even better.

The range will feel very different at first. You're launching balls into the distance rather than watching them roll to a nearby target. But the principles remain the same: you still have a target, and you're still learning control.

Start with four fundamentals that need to become automatic: grip, posture, ball position, and alignment. These are your always-and-forever basics. Get them wired into your motor memory so deeply that you don't have to think about them. (We'll cover these in detail in the next chapter.)

Begin with the short iron. Your body and legs become even more important. Putting is all arms and hands, a full swing is all that and your entire body, Make smooth but free swings—don't stab at the ball or try to hit as hard as you can. Feel the rhythm throughout your body. Keep your balance. As you start to get it, work your way up to the mid-iron, then the hybrid. Don't tire yourself out by hitting too many shots. Just 4 or 5 per club at first. If you cycle through those clubs and still feel good, start over with the short iron and work up again.

There's no rush to get to the driver. In fact, the longer you wait, the better your driver swing will be when you finally get there. Wait until the other clubs feel comfortable before you pick it up. When you do, start with practice swings to feel the length and weight, then make the same smooth motion you've been building with the shorter clubs.

Keep your short game practice alive during this phase. For every range session, spend equal time around the greens. That balance will serve you well.

Play Your First Round

You're ready to play when the fundamentals feel comfortable and you're hitting the ball with reasonable consistency. Not perfectly—no one does—but well enough that you understand cause and effect.

Start on a par 3 course. Your goal isn't a score—in fact, don't keep score. Experience the rhythm of actual play: walking, club selection, dealing with different lies, reading the course, managing your emotions when things don't go as planned. You will do a lot of chipping and putting, but you're ready for that. The key word is observe.

If you can, take a lesson or two around this time. A good instructor can spot issues in your fundamentals before they become ingrained. But you'll arrive with a foundation—you already know how to putt, chip, and make contact. The instructor will probably refine, rather than rebuild.

You started in the shallow end. Now you know how to swim. Build from the hole backward and you'll be in a stronger position to progress and enjoy the game for years to come.

All good swings start with The Core 4. Make these second nature and the club becomes an extension of your intention rather than a source of uncertainty.

The Core 4

A fluid, powerful golf swing conforms to the laws of biomechanics and motor control. These principles are as fixed as gravity. But golfers come in all shapes and sizes, which means there can't be just one correct way to swing that works for everyone.

What is universal is the requirement for a proper setup. This is the final analytical preparation phase before you turn your swing over to your intuitive mind.

The Basis for Every Good Swing

The success of every great golf shot—from a 250-yard drive to a delicate putt—is built on the foundation of the Core 4. **Grip**, **posture**, **ball position** and **alignment**.

They will remain constant throughout your swing, which makes it critical for you to get them right, check them, adjust them as needed, and lock them in, **before** every shot. When you build your checklist, The Core 4 must be on it. Always start a practice session with the Core 4.

Feel the 4

Although this is your analytical mind at work, your intuitive mind, must be engaged as well. Learn to recognize what feels right when the elements are set properly. Pay close attention as you settle into them and learn to recognize when something feels off and have the discipline to stop and reset. Below is my thought process and how I build my setup. But every golfer is different. Consider this only a starting point, and I recommend working with a certified instructor who can tailor guidance to your specific needs.

Grip: Your Connection to the Club

Your grip is your only physical connection to the club. Small deviations from your established grip pattern can produce dramatic changes in ball flight. Check and recheck it.

The two most popular grips among professionals are the overlapping grip and the interlocking grip, with pro golfers split fairly evenly between them.

Left Hand (for right-handed golfers)

Place the grip diagonally across your left hand, running from the tip of your index finger to where your little finger meets your palm. Close your hand around the shaft with firm but relaxed pressure.

Right Hand

For the overlapping grip, rest your right pinky on top of your left hand, letting it settle between your left index and middle fingers. For the interlocking grip, weave your right pinky under your left index finger, interlocking the two fingers together. Either way, your hands should feel unified, working as a single unit.

The Visual Check

Looking down at your hands as you address the ball, your right thumb and index finger should form a "V" pointing toward your right shoulder. You should see two knuckles on your left hand—this is a "neutral" grip.

More than two knuckles showing creates a "strong" grip that tends to close the clubface, producing a draw bias. Fewer than two knuckles creates a "weak" grip that tends to open the clubface, producing a fade bias. If you consistently slice, your left hand grip may be too weak—strengthen it by showing more knuckles. If you hook the ball, try weakening your grip slightly by showing fewer knuckles.

A proper grip might not feel comfortable initially. You'll naturally drift toward what feels familiar rather than what produces good results. Check your grip before every shot to prevent this invisible drift.

Grip Pressure

Hold the club firmly enough that it won't slip, but lightly enough that you can feel the texture of the grip. Sam Snead described it as holding a live bird—with just enough pressure that the bird can't fly away, but not so tightly that the bird can't breathe. Excessive grip tension travels up your arms into your shoulders, disrupting tempo and timing.[56]

Posture: Athletic and Ready

Good golf posture mirrors athletic posture in other sports. Think of a shortstop ready for a ground ball or a basketball player preparing to defend—balanced, alert, ready to move.

To set your posture, hold any club horizontally in front of you at chest height with your feet shoulder-width apart. Bend forward from your hips—not your waist—while flexing your knees slightly. Then lower the club until the clubhead touches the ground.

You now have proper golf posture. The clubhead resting on the ground shows you the correct distance from the ball. Your weight should be balanced and slightly favoring the balls of your feet, with your rear end positioned over your heels.

Shorter clubs position you closer to the ball. Longer clubs position you further away. The posture process remains the same.

Ball Position: The Key to Solid Contact

The clubhead reaches its lowest point somewhere between your feet when you swing. Where this low point occurs determines the quality of contact and depends largely on the club you're using.

Driver

Position the ball about an inch inside your left heel (for right-handed golfers). The driver should contact the ball on the upswing, after the clubhead has passed its lowest point. This ascending strike creates optimal launch angle and maximizes distance.

Irons

Position the ball in the center of your stance. Irons should strike the ball on the downswing, before reaching the lowest point. This compresses the ball against the turf for optimal trajectory and spin. Hit the ball first, then turf.

Fairway Woods and Hybrids

Position the ball slightly forward of center—between your iron and driver positions. These clubs should also contact the ball on a descending blow, but less steeply than irons.

Understanding where the clubhead reaches its lowest point for each club type allows you to position the ball for clean, consistent contact.

Alignment: Aim Small, Miss Small

Unlike archery and rifle shooting, golfers don't face the target directly. We stand to the side and align our body parallel to the target line—like standing on railroad tracks, with the ball on one rail and our feet on the other.

Start by selecting your target and establishing your grip. Place the clubhead behind the ball and square it to the target line, keeping your feet close together. Step your front foot forward into position, then step your back foot into position appropriate for the club and shot.

The most reliable way to verify target alignment is the thigh test. Place a club across both thighs—where the club points is where your body is aimed. This puts you in proper alignment parallel to your target line.

But physical alignment is only half the equation. Your mind must also be aligned with your intention. Sometimes, after setting up perfectly, a stray thought about a hazard or previous bad shot can sabotage your commitment. If negative thoughts creep in, step back, let them pass, and reset both your physical and mental alignment. Without this recalibration, distracting thoughts can take over during the swing and work at cross purposes with your intended target.

Once your setup is complete, your analytical mind has done its job. Club chosen. Setup established. Target confirmed. Alignment complete. Everything from this point forward should be controlled by your intuitive mind.

The Full Swing

You've built your foundation. Now put it in motion. The Core 4 gave you structure. The full swing gives you action. This is where static becomes dynamic—where golf begins.

The full swing is at the crossroads of distance and direction. It's how you cover the vast majority of the course—hole after hole. This is where mental preparation and physical execution unite.

Golf's Beautiful Paradox

Your putting can make or break your score, yet putts are the shortest shots. Meanwhile, full swings travel far but consume almost no time during a round. The average golfer putts about 150 yards per round. On a 6,000-yard course, that's 2.5% of the total distance. The other 5,850 yards are generated from full or modified swings.

A pure drive can carry 250 yards or more. A tap-in putt rolls 4 inches. Both count as one stroke. Every swing matters. This is why developing a reliable, repeatable swing built on the Core 4 is essential to the physical game.

One swing lasts about 1.5 seconds. In a four-hour round where you shoot 85, your total swing time adds up to roughly 2 minutes. Less than 1% of the entire round.

You spend less than 1% of your round swinging a club. The other 99% is where golf is actually played—between your ears, between your shots. That mental space is either working for you or against you. There is no neutral. The Swing to Flow process gives you a ways to use that 99%—quieting the analytical mind, staying present, and preparing your intuitive mind to take over when it's time to swing.

The 3:1 Ratio

Most backswings take roughly three times longer than the downswing. In a typical swing, the backswing might consume just over a second while the downswing takes less than half a second. This natural rhythm makes sense—you're winding up and storing power on the backswing, then releasing it explosively through the downswing. This slower-back, faster-through tempo creates power. Feel it, don't count it.

Work with an Instructor

I encourage everyone who is serious about playing golf regularly to have a PGA certified instructor observe you and offer feedback to refine your swing. The golf swing is complicated and happens so quickly which is one of the reasons it's so hard to repeat.

As you work with an instructor and build your swing, it's important to strengthen your golf consciousness along with your mechanics.

Watch the Pros

There are ample opportunities to watch touring pros; televised tournaments, streaming services, even YouTube. When I watch an elite player swing, I observe their tempo. Tempo is the soul of the golf swing. Tempo isn't swing speed. Some players swing fast, others slow—both can have good tempo. Tempo is the smooth, synchronized rhythm that flows from backswing through downswing, keeping everything on path and preventing the swing from falling apart. It's like music.

The Magical Transition

One of my favorite things to watch for in a quality golf swing is that split second before the backswing completely finishes. At that instant, something remarkable happens: the body starts rotating toward the target while the arms are still completing the backswing. The golfer is *moving backward and forward* at the same time. The body leads the downswing; the arms and hands follow. View this slow motion video[1] of Tiger Woods swinging a 3-wood at the British Open to see this executed perfectly.[57]

Think Motion, Not Shot

Stop trying to hit shots. Make motions instead. Here's why this matters: a shot is a result. A motion is a process. When you describe any golf shot, you're really describing the motion that created it. That's why golf analysts on TV say, "Let's look at that shot" then show it in super slow motion.

By thinking motion instead of shot, you prepare your mind for the swing, not some future outcome. This subtle mental shift promotes freedom, crisper tempo, and eliminates the urge to control or manipulate mid-swing.

Homer Kelley, author of *The Golfing Machine*, said it perfectly: "Learn feel from mechanics *rather* than mechanics from feel" (emphasis in original).[58] Build the foundation with proper mechanics. Then let feel take over. That's when golf becomes a joy.

How Hard Do You Swing?

On normal shots, I swing at 75% of my power, on longer shots I swing at 90%. If I go all out, I do not make solid contact—which is the most important thing. —Tiger Woods[59]

Going all out on any swing is ill-advised. The risk is too great that you'll mishit the shot. So what should your swing effort be? Smooth, with good tempo. A swing where you maintain your balance through the follow-through. If you lose your balance, the first place to look is

---

1. https://www.youtube.com/watch?v=R3jDc2eUepg

your swing speed. Don't rush the downswing. Let your intuitive mind deliver tempo and balance through the finish. When you can do that consistently, power takes care of itself.

The Quiet Eye

Where your eyes go, your mind follows. Yet most golfers never consider what they're looking at, or for how long, before starting their swing. When I ask golfers what their eyes were focused on just before they swing, there's always a pause. Most of them say they don't know.

The Quiet Eye method shifts visual attention from a source of interference into a foundation for intuitive execution. It works by doing something elegantly simple: giving your eyes one clear job before you swing.

Dr. Joan Vickers, a Canadian professor and researcher at the University of Calgary, studied elite golfers in the 1980s and '90s using advanced camera technology and sensors. She observed that elite golfers maintain their gaze on the back of the ball significantly longer than recreational players—typically 2.5 to 3.0 seconds compared to just 1.0 to 1.5 seconds for amateurs. This extended visual focus reorganizes how the brain controls the golf motion on all shots, from full swings to putting. She named it the Quiet Eye method.[60]

If your eyes are constantly darting from one place to another while preparing for a shot, you are creating visual instability. This causes attention to fragment, disrupting tempo. Visual jumping is intrusion. Visual stillness is trust. Keep your eyes locked on an exact spot as you start your swing. No mental wandering. Just steady visual focus on that single point.

Here's what's happening: your analytical mind is still active during execution, searching for information, checking position, trying to control outcomes. This interference can prevent your intuitive mind from doing what it does naturally—executing the motion smoothly based on clear, stable visual input.

If you find yourself looking at your club as you start the backswing, this also inhibits your intuitive mind. Harvey Penick reminds us, "Watching the clubhead go back is a terrible habit."[61]

One word of caution. If you focus so long that you're still doing it through downswing and impact, you will disrupt your natural motion and might end up swinging mostly with your arms, which will kill your speed. It's a fine line. The Quiet Eye does not work for all golfers. Try it, but don't force it.

Your swing is yours—unique, evolving, and built on a foundation of mechanics, mindfulness, and trust. But that swing doesn't exist in isolation. It's delivered through the clubs in your bag, and the right tools make a difference.

Tools of the Trade

Each club in your bag has a specific purpose but can be used in multiple ways depending on the shot you face. Practice with every club you carry. We all have a favorite club we trust completely. That's great, but don't neglect the ones that give you trouble. If you don't practice with a club, don't use it during play. Better yet, remove it from your bag and replace it with one you will actually use.

Golf equipment has evolved and continues to evolve dramatically. In 1913, Francis Ouimet won the US Open with just seven clubs. By 1935, players were carrying up to 32 clubs before the USGA limited the number to fourteen in 1939.

Of course the player matters more than the club, but I strongly urge anyone buying a new set to get professionally fitted. Modern technology allows precise swing analysis, and only a skilled professional can translate those insights into personalized club specifications. The cost is minimal—many shops won't charge fitting fees if you purchase from them. In golf, every legal advantage should be taken.

Don't feel pressured to carry a specific mix of woods, hybrids, irons, or wedges. Your bag should evolve with your game. "Carry what you can hit" is a good motto, but ensure you have enough variety to handle different situations without creating unnecessary disadvantages. You can change clubs based on the course you're playing.

Here's something many golfers don't realize: clean clubs perform better. Of course you wipe off the clubface, but you must scrape the grime out of the grooves of irons. No grooves, no spin. Regarding grips—you will see the pros constantly wiping them down during play. They get sweaty and grimy, which affects feel and control. Clean them.

The right equipment matters, but it only helps if you're ready to use it.

Great golf doesn't emerge from chaos—it emerges from a mind that's free to focus. That starts with how you organize your game before you ever address the ball.

Organized Golf

I was recently paired with a young man eager to get on the course—confident he was ready to play. His cart contained two cigars, a lighter, car keys, cellphone, wireless speaker, and a rangefinder with a dead battery. He also had his clubs, but as we drove to the first tee, his bag fell off the cart. To quote Yogi Berra, "We're lost, but we're making good time."

Golfers may think organization is about being neat or disciplined. They may see it as something separate from the creative, intuitive side of the game. But what if organization is actually a prerequisite to attaining a state of flow? What if being disorganized is preventing you from experiencing your best golf?

The greatest golfers make the game look effortless because they've organized everything that can be organized. They've built reliable external systems because they know unnecessary disruption adds to distraction. You can build those systems too. Here's how.

The Foundation Beneath the Flow

The more organized your external world, the freer your internal world becomes. Flow states don't emerge from chaos—they arise from a foundation so solid that your conscious mind can let go and allow intuition to take over.

The Mental Cost of Disorganization

Every unmade decision, every misplaced item, every uncertainty creates what psychologists call "cognitive load." When you're searching for a tee while standing on the box, or a ball mark after you've made your first putt, you're spending mental currency that could be invested in the next shot.

Disorganization creates a constant background hum of anxiety—the opposite of mindfulness, pulling you away from the present moment. Professional golfers understand this instinctively. Watch them on tour: everything has its place, every routine is repeatable, every detail is managed. This isn't obsessive behavior; it's liberation through preparation.

Establish Pre-Round Rituals

Flow states require a transition from your everyday mind to your golf mind. Consistent rituals create repeatable bridges. Arrive at the same time before you tee off, perform the same warm-up sequence, include both technical and feel shots. There is power in ritual. Your body and mind learn the signal: "We're entering golf mode now."

The Phone Problem

This is why it's crucial to resist the temptation to drift into random streams of consciousness that occur when we check our phones during play. Phones are the ultimate distraction device. Sherry Turkle, a noted psychologist at MIT, warns: "Because of our phones, we are forever elsewhere. We're never fully present." Leave it in your bag and unburden yourself from the programming on your screen.

Use Your Checklist

The most important organization in golf happens in the 30-60 seconds before each shot. A consistent pre-shot routine is the gateway to presence. In The Flow Score chapter you created a pre-shot checklist, tested it on the range and during play, and made any necessary adjustments. It's your mental north star. Use it before every shot.

Organize Your Thinking Between Shots

Have a system: Give yourself 5-10 seconds to observe the outcome of a shot, then let it go. In the Mindfulness chapter we learned to calmly acknowledge feelings, thoughts and bodily sensations—without judgment.

Maintain your present-moment awareness as you approach your ball and begin reading the next shot. This behavior creates clear emotional compartments and preserves energy for the next moments that matter.

Maintain Physical Organization

A clean, orderly golf bag signals to your subconscious: "I am in control. I am prepared." Clubs returned to the same place, tees and balls in dedicated pockets, glove always clipped in the same spot. This may seem trivial, but each time you fumble for something, you risk breaking flow. Over 18 holes, these moments accumulate into significant mental fatigue.

Physical organization supports mindfulness. When you play in an organized system, you perform small, intentional actions rather than random searches. *Intention is the essence of mindfulness.*

Organization as Self-Respect

At its deepest level, being organized in golf says: "My time is valuable. My mental energy is precious. I deserve to show up fully prepared to do my best."

When you organize your external world, you create internal spaciousness. Your mind isn't cluttered with logistics—it's clear, present, and available. Intuition can speak clearly.

Control What You Can Control

Organization focuses your energy on what you *can* control and frees you from anxiety about what you *can't*. Being organized is mindfulness—fully engaged with what is, not worried about what might be.

You control your preparation, routine, equipment and response to each shot. You don't control where the ball goes (maybe someday), what score you shoot, or the conditions.

From Organization to Liberation

Liberation is organization's gift: it frees you from your thinking mind. When you trust your routine to handle the process, you don't have to think about the process.

Organization clears the mental space. Now fill it with strategy. A prepared, present mind is exactly what you need for the analytical work ahead—reading the course, managing risk, and making decisions that play to your strengths.

Course Management

Perfect golf doesn't exist. Even tour professionals—machines of consistency by amateur standards—miss fairways, greens, and putts. The difference isn't perfection; it's good planning. They minimize costly mistakes through strategic thinking that reframes eighteen holes from hoping for the best into executing a calculated game plan.

Course management is your analytical mind's domain. This is where you gather information, assess conditions, identify danger, and create a strategy that plays to your strengths while protecting against your weaknesses. Do this work well before you stand over the ball—ideally the day before or morning of your round.

The majority of course management is strategy, but for a strategy to be viable it must be informed by what is physically possible—or at the very least, probable. In golf, that means knowing how far you actually hit each club. Not what you think you hit. Not what you hit once on a perfect day. What you hit consistently.

Most golfers are wildly optimistic about their distances. They remember the one 7-iron that carried 165 yards and forget the dozen that came up short at 150. This self-deception costs strokes.

There are two distances that matter: carry distance—where the ball first hits the ground—and total distance including roll. Of the two, carry distance is what you need to know. Why? Because you can predict where the ball lands, not where it bounces.

The only way to find your true carry distances is to measure them. Find an indoor simulator or range that uses quality tracking technology that's professionally calibrated.

Once you are there, take out your wedge and hit five solid shots, noting the carry distance for each. Throw out the longest and shortest, then average the remaining three. That's your carry distance for that club. Repeat with every club in your bag. Write down the yardages and carry them with you while you play.

You now have accurate, reliable data—the foundation for smart course management.

The Three Fundamentals of Course Management

Effective course strategy doesn't require encyclopedic knowledge of every yardage, contour, or pattern. Strip away the complexity and three elements remain:

One: Know Where NOT to Hit It

Identify the penalty areas that destroy scores—out of bounds, water, thick rough, bunkers you can't escape. These are non-negotiable. Avoid them at all costs.

Two: Know Where TO Hit It

Establish clear target zones for every shot. Not vague intentions, but specific landing areas that set up the next shot. Big part of the fairway. Fat part of the green. Don't overthink, these are obvious when looking at a yardage book.

Three: Understand the Green Complex

Know the pin placement and determine the most favorable approach angles before your tee shot. Select your target accordingly. Know the distance of bunkers guarding the green. Learn which tier the hole is cut on the green. Always think ahead to make your next shot as easy as possible.

Everything else—wind calculations, elevation adjustments, pin sheets, detailed yardage books—represents refinement. Focus on these three fundamentals, then add detail as your game develops.

In Between Clubs

This happens frequently. You stripe a drive down the fairway, pull out your rangefinder, and discover the perfect yardage problem: you're caught exactly between a 7-iron and an 8-iron. Neither feels quite right.

Here's how your analytical mind should handle this decision:

If you must clear trouble in front (bunker, water, hazard), take the longer club. The risk of coming up short far outweighs the risk of going long.

If there's no trouble in front but danger behind the green (OB, water, severe slope), take the shorter club and commit to a smooth, full swing. Missing short leaves a manageable chip. Going long creates disaster.

If the green is open front and back with safe misses in both directions, trust your gut. Pick one club, commit completely, and don't second-guess.

Some players try to finesse these situations by taking the longer club and "taking something off it"—swinging at 80% power to dial in the perfect distance. This requires exceptional feel and extensive practice. Unless you've spent significant time developing this skill, resist the temptation. Partial swings introduce variables that disrupt tempo and solid contact.

Indecision is the enemy of good swings. Standing over a shot thinking "Is this the right club?" activates your analytical mind during execution—exactly when your intuitive mind should be in control. Make the club decision with confidence, then trust it completely. Number three on my pre-shot checklist is: Commit fully to the shot.

When in doubt, favor the club that keeps you away from trouble.

Building A Strategic Foundation

Your analytical mind thrives on information. Before playing a course, understand its character:

Environmental Factors

Prevailing wind direction and strength influence club selection throughout your round. Altitude affects distance—sometimes dramatically. Morning dew slows greens early; afternoon winds pick up as temperatures rise. Course firmness or softness determines how your ball reacts on landing.

Design Philosophy

Every course reveals the architect's defensive strategy. Some designers demand precision through narrow fairways and tight landing zones. Others rely on punishing rough or strategic hazard placement to protect par. Understanding what the architect is trying to make you do—and what they're trying to prevent—lets you play the course on your terms rather than theirs.

Hole-Specific Details

Tactical thinking is needed here. Par and yardage establish the baseline, but hole shape—straight or dogleg—determine optimal positioning. Elevation changes affect club selection. Hazard locations become calculation points you must account for on every shot.

The green complex demands particular attention since this is where scores are determined. Green size and shape influence your margin for error. Understanding slope direction helps you position approach shots that leave makeable putts. Knowing where the safe miss areas are located saves strokes when your approach isn't perfect.

But here's the critical point: All this analysis happens well *before* the shot. Once you step onto the tee, your preparation should be complete.

Tools for Better Decisions

As you apply the Swing to Flow process, your ball striking will become more consistent, boosting confidence. Your scores will improve and the spread between your low rounds and high rounds will shorten. Instead of eight or ten strokes separating them, it will be three or four. This is a major accomplishment.

Once you hit that milestone, you may want to adopt additional tools and thought processes to improve outcomes. Pros avail themselves of as many tools as they can. If it can take even one stroke off their expected round, they'll try it.

Expanding your golf toolkit is not as difficult as you might think. From an expense perspective it's next to nothing. But there is a mental cost. Next-level work becomes additive, shifting from preparation to game-time decision-making increases cognitive load.

If you watch tour players, you'll see them hit a drive 300 yards down the middle of the fairway, leaving a hundred yards to the hole. You expect them to grab a club and instantly make a swing that lands the ball inside three feet of the hole.

But what often happens is this: Everything slows down. The player looks carefully at the shot. They may even walk to the green to get a better look at the landscape. They consult their pin sheet and yardage book. They have a detailed discussion with their caddie, then think some more. Eventually they select a club and execute.

This is their analytical mind at work, processing data, comparing past experiences to the shot at hand to arrive at a decision in real time. The brain is an amazing computer. It can handle a substantial amount information, so why not give it more to work with?

Pin Sheets provide daily hole location data using numbered zones—typically 1 for front, 2 for middle, 3 for back positions. This information directly impacts club selection and target choice. Some courses use color-coded flags: red for front, white for middle, blue for back. Simple and effective. See Appendix for detailed examples.

Yardage Books offer precise distances from various tee positions, hazard locations, carry requirements, and strategic landing zones. Rather than relying on estimates or basic course markers, yardage books allow for precise planning that accounts for your specific capabilities. See Appendix for detailed examples.

Rangefinders provide accurate yardages that eliminate guesswork. Over the years they've become more affordable and reliable. Look for excellent optics, clear field of view, and rechargeable batteries. Some include slope measurements for better distance control. A rangefinder feeds your analytical mind the data it needs for confident club selection.

Keep in mind that the number your rangefinder gives you is carry distance, NOT carry and roll. Adjust accordingly.

Phone Apps offer satellite views, GPS tracking, and detailed hole information. While powerful, they demand significant mental energy and create distractions. I don't use them—no phones on the course—and don't recommend them for developing golfers. Players often spend more time managing their app than preparing for shots. The technology is impressive, but it fragments focus.

Internal Par: Recalibrating Expectations

Some holes consistently challenge your skill level. That 415-yard par 4 you've never reached in two? Mentally adjust it to a par 5. The well-protected par 3 that routinely produces big numbers? Give it an extra stroke in your mental accounting.

Your scorecard still reflects actual strokes, but the mental shift allows better decisions that align with your capabilities rather than unrealistic expectations that lead to forced shots. Your intuitive mind relaxes. Pressure decreases. Better choices emerge.

Hole-by-Hole Strategy

Every hole requires a strategic approach tailored to its challenges and your abilities. Think backward from the green to optimize each decision. Once you complete a hole, stand on the green and look back to the tee. This gives you a different view of the hole that can reveal insights, such as landing areas or trouble spots that you couldn't readily see from the tee.

Par 3 Strategy

Success on par 3s comes from disciplined decision-making, not aggressive pin-hunting.

Before selecting your club, study the green layout. Does it have tiers? Which tier holds the pin? Where is the trouble?

Most golfers under-club par 3s. Use your actual carry yardages, not total distance. When between clubs, follow the protocol discussed earlier.

Target the fat part of the green unless the pin sits in an easily accessible location. Avoid "sucker pins" tucked near trouble. Consider your miss patterns—if you tend to miss right, aim slightly left of center.

Once you've chosen your club and target, commit fully. No second-guessing. Trust your preparation and make a confident motion. A ball landing in the middle of the green becomes par more often than you think.

Accept that par isn't always realistic, especially on difficult holes. Sometimes the smartest strategy involves a conservative first shot to a safe area, followed by a chip and putt. This approach prevents the big numbers that can derail an otherwise solid round.

Par 4 Strategy

Break the hole into three components: putting, approach shot, tee shot. Plan backward.

Your tee shot should prioritize position over distance. Find the landing zone that provides the best approach angle while avoiding bunkers and hazards. The driver isn't always the answer—use the longest club that keeps you in the fairway and leaves a comfortable approach distance.

On narrow fairways, consider a 3-wood or hybrid for accuracy. On doglegs, favor the corner without cutting too much distance. On uphill holes, keep in mind your approach shot will likely require more club.

Your approach shot requires careful target selection. Aim for the largest part of the green. Only attack pins in accessible locations. Know your carry distances and account for wind, elevation, and green conditions. Guard against going long—most courses punish this more severely than coming up short.

If you use your driver on short par 4s you might land much closer to the green. Often it's smarter to lay back to your favorite wedge distance. On long par 4s over 400 yards, accept that par is difficult and focus on avoiding big numbers.

Play your game. Don't let playing partners' club choices influence your decisions. Stick to shots with high confidence.

The golden rule: two shots anywhere on the green beat one great shot followed by one disaster. Play for the center unless conditions make attacking the smart play.

Par 5 Strategy

Par 5s present the greatest strategic complexity because you take more shots. Your opening shot should establish position, not chase distance.

The second shot often defines the entire hole. Assess whether the green is realistically reachable. If going for it, ensure a miss won't be catastrophic. If laying up proves wiser, choose a distance that leaves your preferred club—not necessarily the closest position to the green.

If you've executed well on the first two shots, your approach should leave you with a high-lofted club in hand. Slow down. Remember your pre-shot checklist. This is where your round can improve significantly or unravel completely.

You now have the complete Swing to Flow system: mechanics, mindfulness, intuition, flow, pre-round preparation, strategic thinking, and techniques for every club and situation. But here's what every serious golfer discovers: knowledge alone isn't enough. Without outside perspective, we drift. Our grips change imperceptibly. Our setups shift. Our swings evolve in ways we can't see. Growth requires more than practice. It requires honest feedback from sources beyond your own perception.

Continuous Improvement

You have the framework, the tools, and the knowledge to transform your game. Now comes the hard truth: none of it matters if you let it drift. Golf skills erode invisibly. Mechanics shift. Mental discipline slips. Even tour professionals—masters of their craft—require constant outside observation to maintain what they've built. You will too.

Everything you've learned creates a foundation. The Swing to Flow framework, mental game tools, technical fundamentals, the Flow Scorecard, course management strategies—these form a complete system for better golf. But systems require maintenance. Skills need refinement. And we all have blind spots we simply cannot see without help.

This final chapter addresses how to sustain and grow what you've built through intelligent use of outside perspective that keeps you centered.

We Need Outside Eyes

Golf swings naturally evolve through imperceptible drift. What feels like a minor adjustment to achieve better contact in practice can gradually morph into a flaw after only a few holes. These changes occur gradually and are often never noticed.

Grip pressure can increase during stressful times. Setup positions shift slightly to compensate for other changes we've unknowingly made in our swing. Tempo changes develop as we unconsciously try to hit the ball farther or revert to swinging from the top. Each of these shifts—and many more—feel normal because they start small but grow incrementally. Their cumulative effect can turn a reliable swing into an unreliable one.

Outside perspective catches these changes before they become ingrained.

The Limitations of Self-Coaching

When we practice alone, we become both student and teacher and tend to reinforce what feels comfortable rather than what produces optimal results. Our internal feedback system, while valuable for tempo and contact, cannot provide the objective analysis needed for technical improvement.

The disconnect between feel and reality creates a fundamental problem: what feels like a significant change might be barely noticeable, while correct positions often feel awkward or extreme. This makes us unreliable judges of our own swing. A few good shots convince us we've solved the problem, while a few bad shots lead us to abandon techniques that weren't actually the issue.

Confirmation bias leads us to notice evidence that supports our current beliefs and ignore signals that contradict them. And we easily miss the forest for the trees, focusing intently on one element while other aspects of our game can go unnoticed.

Outside perspective provides observation unclouded by our biases.

Professional Instruction

Finding the right instructor matters. Look for PGA certification, modern swing analysis capability, clear communication skills, and experience working with golfers at your level. You need someone you feel comfortable with who matches your learning style.

Even golfers with solid fundamentals benefit from periodic check-ins. Schedule pre-season sessions to catch off-season drift before it affects your scores. Book mid-season adjustments when performance plateaus despite consistent practice. Use post-season analysis to plan winter priorities with clear direction.

When you're ready for the next level but aren't sure how to get there, professional guidance provides the roadmap for advancement.

For beginners, one hour with a qualified professional at the start prevents years of fighting bad habits that become increasingly difficult to correct later.

Knowledgeable Playing Partners

A trusted playing partner with solid fundamentals and a good eye can serve as an informal coach—if you establish ground rules. Make feedback optional, not automatic. Focus on one thing at a time. Keep it conversational, not instructional. And ensure the arrangement benefits both players.

The best partnerships involve mutual observation where you learn from watching each other's process as much as from direct feedback. This arrangement works when both players commit to honest, supportive observation without letting golf advice strain the friendship.

Video Analysis

Modern smartphones provide excellent slow-motion capabilities that reveal swing details invisible to the naked eye. To use video effectively, establish consistent camera positions—down-the-line and face-on—and maintain the same distance each time you record. This consistency allows meaningful comparison over time.

Capture multiple swings to identify patterns rather than judging yourself on a single shot. Use your checklist and mental tools when recording. When reviewing footage, compare current swings to previous recordings to spot drift in mechanics. Look for changes in tempo, positions, or sequencing, but resist the urge to analyze everything at once.

Focus on one element per review session and document your observations with dated videos and notes about how each shot felt. This connection between what you see and what you felt builds the self-awareness essential to mindful improvement.

Partner with someone to handle recording so you can focus entirely on hitting shots, or invest in a tripod with a remote trigger for independent sessions.

Performance Technology

Launch monitors and swing analysis software provide objective data that can validate or challenge your perceptions. However, they're expensive and require knowledge to interpret meaningfully. More importantly, constant data monitoring can pull you away from the feel and awareness that mindful golf emphasizes.

Use technology sparingly for occasional check-ins, preferably with professional guidance to understand what the numbers reveal. Let data inform your practice, not dominate it.

The Path Forward

Your journey with Swing to Flow begins now—not when you've mastered everything in this book, but the moment you step onto the course with new awareness. Every round becomes data. Every shot becomes feedback. Every mental score reveals where you're growing and where you need support.

The golfers who improve aren't necessarily the ones with the most talent or the best equipment. They're the ones who stay curious, seek objective feedback, and refuse to drift into comfortable mediocrity. They organize their game. They practice with intention. They stay present. They trust their intuition. And when they lose their way, they ask for help.

Tour players invest in comprehensive support teams—swing coaches, putting coaches, sports psychologists, fitness trainers, nutritionists—because they recognize that outside perspective is essential for maintaining peak performance. The majority of us don't depend on golf for our livelihood, but we share the same need: objective observation that catches what we cannot see ourselves.

I hope some of these concepts will help you play better golf and enjoy it more. Continue practicing your mechanics, but also devote some time to cultivating your mental game. The integration of mechanics, mindfulness, and intuition in pursuit of flow.

The course is waiting. Go play.

Afterword

As I write these final words on a pristine Arizona morning, I can see in my mind the first foursome of the day making their way down the fairway. They move with that familiar rhythm all golfers know—the purposeful walk between shots, the pause for consideration, the setup, the swing, and then that moment of suspended attention as the ball arcs through the desert air. Thinking of them, I'm reminded of why I began this book in the first place.

Golf has given me countless gifts over five decades of play. It has tested me, humbled me, frustrated me beyond measure, and yet continues to call me back with the promise of that one pure shot, that one perfect round that exists just beyond reach. But the greatest gift golf has given me wasn't a trophy or a personal best score—it was the discovery that the game's deepest rewards come not from conquering the course, but from harmonizing with it.

When I started playing, I was taught that golf was about mechanics. Fix the swing, lower the score—simple. Decades later, I now understand that mechanics matter, but they're the vessel—the magic happens when we stop trying to control and start creating conditions for our best golf to emerge by allowing our golf consciousness to participate in the process.

This book represents my attempt to share what I've learned about that delicate dance between knowing and trusting, between preparation and presence, between the analytical mind that plans each shot and the intuitive mind that executes it. If you've made it this far, you've likely recognized something in these pages that resonates with your own experience—those moments when everything clicked, when the club felt weightless in your hands, when the ball seemed to know exactly where to go.

The Journey Continues

Swing to Flow is an ongoing practice. Some days you'll step onto the first tee and feel that familiar harmony between mind and body from your very first swing. Other days, it will elude you entirely, leaving you to wonder if you've ever truly played this game before. This is golf's way of keeping us humble, keeping us learning, keeping us present.

As you continue your own golf journey, I encourage you to be patient with the process. Developing a strong golf consciousness takes time. Your analytical mind, so accustomed to being in charge, won't easily step aside to let intuition lead. There will be rounds where you revert to old patterns, where mechanical thoughts crowd out presence, where fear overrides trust. This is normal. This is human. This is golf.

But there will also be those transcendent moments—perhaps an entire hole, maybe even a full nine—where you'll experience what it means to truly play in the flow. When they arrive, don't try to analyze them. Simply experience them. Let them teach you what's possible when mechanics and mindfulness work in perfect partnership.

A Personal Note

Throughout this book, I've shared techniques and insights gathered from decades of play, study, and observation. But I'm still learning. Every round teaches me something new about the game and about myself.

This is why I continue to practice both the physical and mental aspects of the game. Each morning's meditation isn't only preparation for golf—it's preparation for life. The mindfulness we develop on the course doesn't stay there. It follows us home, into our relationships, our work, our quiet moments of reflection. Golf becomes a moving meditation, a four-hour practice in presence that has the power to enrich every aspect of our lives.

Your Own Path

While I've offered you a framework, remember that your path to a stronger golf consciousness will be uniquely your own. You might find that visualization comes naturally while tempo remains elusive. Perhaps your short game flows effortlessly while your driver demands constant attention. Honor these differences. Work with them rather than against them.

Consider keeping a golf journal, not just of scores and statistics, but of feelings and insights. Note those moments when you felt truly present. Document what conditions—internal and external—seemed to facilitate flow. Over time, patterns will emerge, and you'll develop a better understanding of what it takes to access your best golf.

And please, be kind to yourself in this process. Golf is hard enough without adding self-criticism to the challenge. Every professional has days when they can't find the fairway. Every amateur has moments of brilliance. The beauty of golf lies not in perfection but in the endless opportunity for growth, discovery, and those fleeting moments of pure, effortless excellence.

Each shot is a new beginning, a fresh opportunity to apply what we've learned, to trust what we know, to let go of what we can't control. The scorecard will archive our numbers, but it can't capture the feeling of a perfectly struck iron shot, the satisfaction of a well-read putt, or the simple joy of walking a beautiful course on a perfect day with your friends.

My hope is that this book helps you find more of those moments—not just the ones where the ball goes where you intended, but the ones where you were so fully present, so completely absorbed in the process, that the outcome becomes secondary to the experience itself. Trust the process. Trust your preparation. Most importantly, trust yourself.

A Final Thought

As I prepare to head out for my next round, I'm reminded of something Ben Hogan once said: "The most important shot in golf is the next one." This wisdom extends beyond the course. The most important moment in life is the next one. The present one. This. One. Now.

I'll leave you with this: somewhere out there is your perfect round. It's not waiting for you to develop a flawless swing or to master every possible shot. It's waiting for you to show up fully—mechanics prepared, mind present, intuition engaged, ready to flow with whatever the course presents.

Appendix

Many courses provide pin sheets in print or through their app. The example below uses four zones for precise target selection. Each diagram shows green shape, bunkers, tiers, swales, and exact dimensions in yards.

Before teeing off, find the pin location for your round. Scan the sheet and note any difficult holes or ones that typically give you trouble.

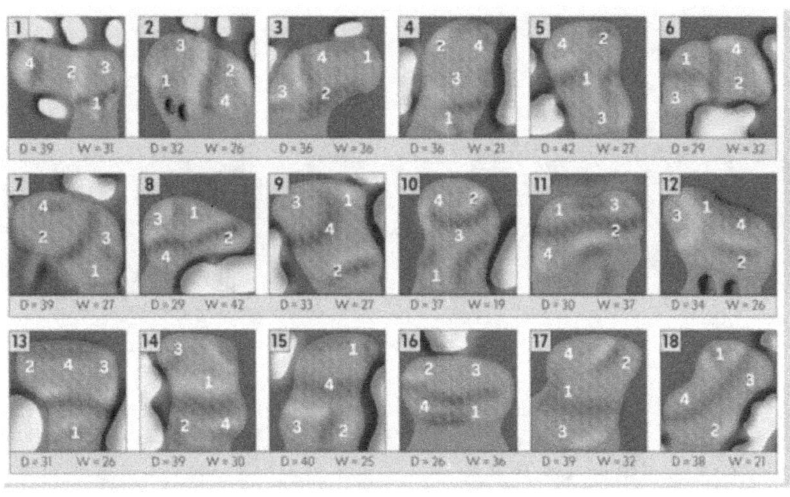

Pin Sheet: The Clubs at Arrowhead, King Course, Glendale, AZ

Yardage Maps

Quality yardage maps provide course layout diagrams, approach shot information, hazard locations with distances, and green complexes with surrounding features. The professionals use StrackaLine books—exceptional detail but more data than most recreational golfers need. I use maps produced by Putt View: affordable, clear, and practical for on-course use. The green charts are amazing. They of course help with putting, but I also use them when selecting a landing area that will give me an uphill putt.

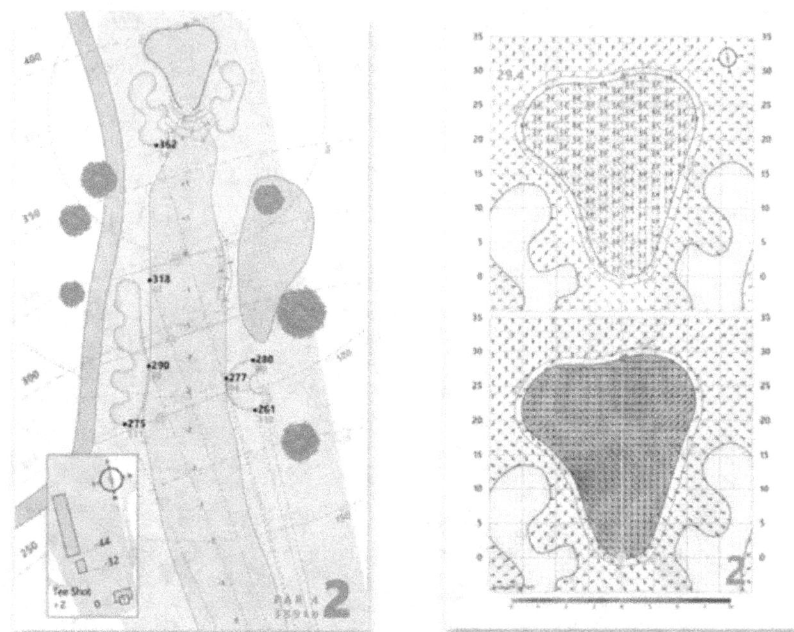

Sample pages from Putt View yardage book

How to Use These Tools

The real power emerges when you view pin sheets and yardage maps together. This combination gives your analytical mind the information it needs to create a complete strategy before your intuitive mind executes the shot. Let's examine two holes from my home course and walk through how yardage maps help plan hole strategy.

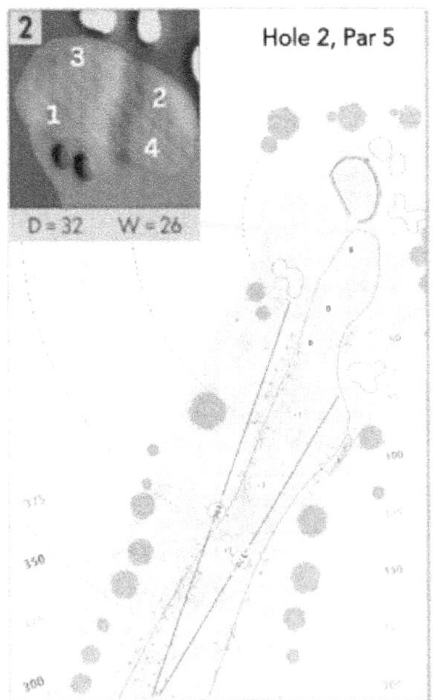

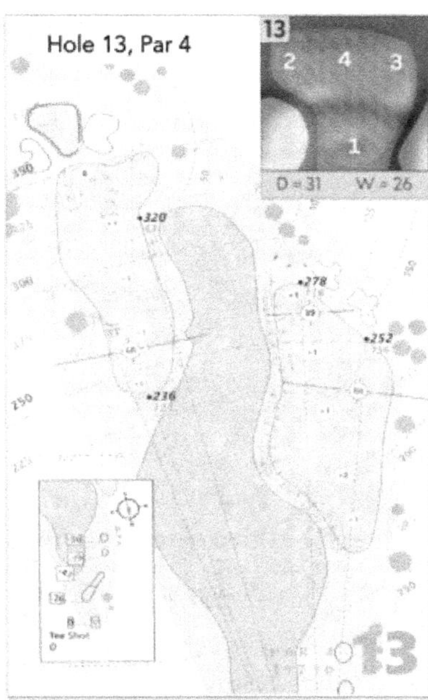

Hole 2, Par 5

Looking at the yardage map, we immediately notice three bunker shapes behind and right of the green, with two dark-colored ovals in the front left. These are grass hollows—also called swales. Not as difficult to navigate as bunkers, but you risk an uneven lie. Since it's a par 5, you'll most likely hit a high lofted club into this green as your third shot, increasing your control ability.

Another data point to consider is green depth and width. This green measures 32 yards deep and 26 yards wide—a depth-to-width ratio of 16:13, meaning the green is nearly as deep as it is wide. This oval shape makes it easier to identify a safe landing area.

Pin left: Target the left half of the green. Calculate your carry to land

5-10 yards short of the back bunker—safely past the hollows but short of trouble. Miss left and you have a routine chip shot. Miss right and you have an uphill putt.

Pin right: Target the center of the green. Distance calculation becomes trickier because the right bunker is much closer to this pin position, though you have no swales to clear. The smart choice is to play for the front edge—short leaves a simple chip, long keeps you on the putting surface.

Hole 13, Par 4

This green has two distinct tiers. Looking at the green detail zones 2, 3, and 4 sit on the higher tier while zone 1 occupies the lower tier. Two large bunkers protect the front half of the green, one on either side. This green measures 31 yards deep and 26 yards wide—a ratio similar to Hole 2. But this measurement is less useful because the green isn't oval. The back half is very wide while the front narrows dramatically.

This hole—designed by Arnold Palmer—demonstrates why studying pin sheets and yardage maps together is critical. The large water hazard down the center of the hole dominates the landscape, creating two distinct paths to the green from the tee (see the tee shot diagram in the lower left corner.)

Left path: Long carry over water, but offers a clear angle and shorter distance to the green. No bunkers to negotiate.

Right path: No water carry off the tee, but this drastically changes your approach angle. From the right side you'll be forced to carry the right bunker regardless of pin position. The approach shot will also be 15-20 yards longer. Thanks for that, Arnie.

Your tee shot determines your approach strategy. Some days I go left, some right, depending on wind and how well I'm executing my driver swings.

Pro Tip: I printed the pin sheet, cut out each hole, and pasted them onto the corresponding yardage book pages, giving me a complete view.

Matt Fitzpatrick's Yardage Book

He keeps track of every shot on every hole using his custom shorthand code so he can better understand how he played the hole and revisit them when he returns to that course for future tournaments.

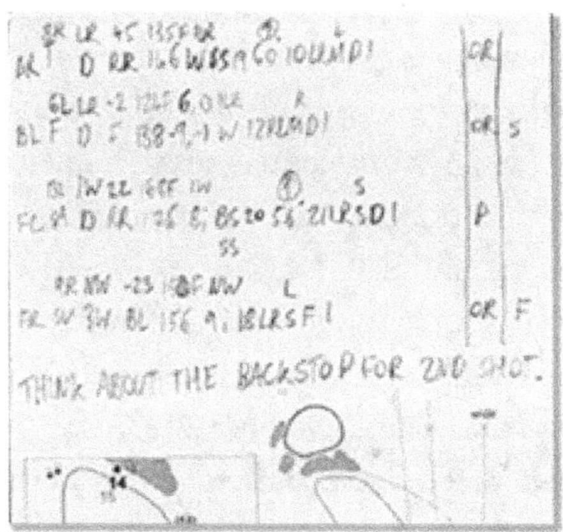

Download and Print the Flow Scorecard and Analytics Spreadsheet

At **swingtoflow.com** click on the **Downloads** link in the top right hand corner. From there download the Excel file.

Notes

1. *How to Play Your Best Golf All the Time* (1953), Tommy Armour, https://www.youtube.com/watch?v=z3m8_C5YgX4.

2. *A New Way to Better Golf* (1933) Alex Morrison, Archive.org, page V, https://archive.org/details/newwaytobettergo00morr/page/n5/mode/2up.

3. *Harvey Penick's Little Red Book, Lessons and Teachings from a Lifetime in Golf* (1992), Harvey Penick with Bud Shrake, page 103.

4. *The Wisdom of Jack*, Golf Digest, article not dated, https://www.golfdigest.com/story/the-wisdom-of-jack.

5. *Understanding the Golfers at Your Course*, USGA (2022), https://www.usga.org/content/usga/home-page/course-care/green-section-record/60/12/understanding-the-golfers-at-your-course.html.

6. The National Golf Foundation, golf industry facts, https://www.ngf.org/the-clubhouse/golf-industry-research/.

7. Golf Digest magazine, October 2023, https://www.golfdigest.com/story/the-50-golf-books-every-golfer-should-read.

8. *Glotta: A Poem* by James Arbuckle (1721), Archive.org, https://archive.org/details/bim_eighteenth-century_glotta-a-poem-humbly-ins_arbuckle-james_1721/mode/2up.

9. Scottish Golf History website lists early books related to golf at https://www.scottishgolfhistory.org/references-2/oldest-golf-histories/.

10. *Homer Kelley's Golfing Machine: The Curious Quest that Solved Golf* (2009), Scott Gummer, Gotham Books, pages 1-9.

11. *The Golfing Machine: Geometric Golf: The Computer Age*

Approach to Golfing Perfection Homer Kelley (1969), Edition 7.2, (2006), page 1.

12. *The Golfing Machine: Geometric Golf: The Computer Age Approach to Golfing Perfection* Homer Kelley (1969), Edition 7.2, (2006), page 232.

13. *Golf Swing Biomechanics: A Systematic Review and Methodological Recommendations for Kinematics*, National Library of Medicine, https://pmc.ncbi.nlm.nih.gov/articles/PMC9227529/.

14. "Procedural Memory," ScienceDirect Topics (2025). The article reviews research showing procedural memory relies on a network including the basal ganglia, premotor cortex, cerebellum, and inferior parietal cortex. https://www.sciencedirect.com/topics/neuroscience/procedural-memory

15. "Motor Memory," ScienceDirect Topics (2025). Reviews evidence that motor memory storage involves the principal circuits that mediate behavioral motor patterns, including motor cortex, basal ganglia, and spinal cord motor neurons. https://www.sciencedirect.com/topics/psychology/motor-memory

16. Shohamy, D., Myers, C.E., Grossman, S., Sage, J., Gluck, M.A., & Poldrack, R.A., "The role of the basal ganglia in learning and memory: Insight from Parkinson's disease," *Neuroscience & Biobehavioral Reviews* (2004). Findings in animals and humans indicate the basal ganglia contribute to incremental learning of stimulus-response associations. https://pmc.ncbi.nlm.nih.gov/articles/PMC3772079/

17. Berlot, E., Popp, N.J., & Diedrichsen, J., "A critical re-evaluation of fMRI signatures of motor sequence learning," *eLife* (May 13, 2020). Systematic assessment reveals widespread activity reductions and subtle pattern changes

outside primary motor cortex as motor skills develop. https://elifesciences.org/articles/55241

18. "Motor Learning," ScienceDirect Topics (2025). Reviews neuroimaging evidence showing overall reduction in brain activity as learning progresses, indicating increased neural efficiency. https://www.sciencedirect.com/topics/neuroscience/motor-learning

19. Ghilardi, M.F., Moisello, C., Silvestri, G., Ghez, C., & Krakauer, J.W., "The many facets of motor learning and their relevance for Parkinson's disease," *Frontiers in Neurology* (July 2017). Describes the smooth transition from visual-cognitive to motor loop, from anterior to posterior circuits, and from declarative learning to optimization networks. https://pmc.ncbi.nlm.nih.gov/articles/PMC5486221/

20. Ullman, M.T., "The Declarative/Procedural Model," in *Neurobiology of Language* (2016). The procedural memory system, including basal ganglia and cerebellum, underlies learning and execution of motor and cognitive skills, especially sequences. https://www.sciencedirect.com/topics/neuroscience/procedural-memory

21. See note 16.

22. Kleynen, M., et al., "Motor Learning," in *Neurorehabilitation Technology* (2025). Distinguishes implicit motor learning governed by procedural memory (unconscious) from explicit motor learning involving conscious recollection (declarative memory). https://www.sciencedirect.com/topics/neuroscience/motor-learning

23. See note 15.

24. Author's definition of golf mechanics.

25. Tiger Woods quote from a video interview posted on Golf State of Mind (2010), https://golfstateofmind.com/inside-the-golfing-brain-of-tiger-woods/.

26. *The Shohei Ohtani Rules: Handling a Two-Way Experiment With Care*, article by Billy Wiltz, The New York Times (2018), https://www.nytimes.com/2018/04/27/sports/shohei-ohtani-los-angeles-angels.html.

27. Shohei Ohtani Discusses The Mental Challenges of Being a Two-Way Player, Phil Nevin, Sports Illustrated via the Orange County Register (2023), https://www.si.com/mlb/angels/angels-news/angels-have-changed-course-on-managerial-search-report.

28. Author's definition of mindfulness.

29. *Mindfulness and Awareness: The Core of Golf Teaching*, themindofgolf.com (2017), https://themindofgolf.com/mindfulness-and-awareness/.

30. *The History and Origins of Mindfulness*, PositivePsychology.com (2017), https://positivepsychology.com/history-of-mindfulness/.

31. *What's the Background of Mindfulness?* Psychcentral.com, article not dated, https://psychcentral.com/lib/a-brief-history-of-mindfulness-in-the-usa-and-its-impact-on-our-lives.

32. *Mindfulness Practice Leads to Increases in Regional Brain Gray Matter Density*, National Library of Medicine, National Center for Biotechnology Information, PubMed Central (2012), https://pmc.ncbi.nlm.nih.gov/articles/PMC3004979/.

33. *Neurobiological Changes Induced by Mindfulness and Meditation: A Systematic Review* (2024), Silvio Ionta and Hideya Kawasaki, mdpi.com, https://www.mdpi.com/2227-9059/12/11/2613.

34. *Sports Psychology History*, psychology.iresearchnet.com, https://psychology.iresearchnet.com/sports-psychology/sports-psychology-history/.

35. *Sports Psychology,* Wikipedia.org, https://en.wikipedia.org/wiki/Sport_psychology.

36. *An Assessment of the Use of Imagery by Elite Athletes: Athlete, Coach and Sports Psychologists Perspectives* (1989), by D.P. Jowdy, S.M. Murphy and S.K. Durtschi. This was an internal research report by the U.S. Olympic Committee and since it was not peer-reviewed, it is harder to access the full document. It does have widespread acceptance as foundational evidence of the prevalence of mental imagery techniques.

37. *The Inner Game of Golf,* Timothy Gallwey (1979), PDF Summary on shortform.com, https://www.shortform.com/pdf/the-inner-game-of-golf-pdf-w-timothy-gallwey?utm_source=google&utm_medium=pmax&utm_campa yTMvU&gclid=EAIaIQobChMI2rXpq4uzkAMVYChECB3fEh

38. *A Brief History of Meditation*, Mindworks, article not dated, https://mindworks.org/blog/history-origins-of-meditation/.

39. *Meditation*, Cleveland Clinic (2022) https://my.clevelandclinic.org/health/articles/17906-meditation.

40. *The Golfing Machine: Geometric Golf: The Computer Age Approach to Golfing Perfection* Homer Kelley (1969), Edition 7.2, (2006), page 1.

41. Insight Timer, available in the App store and Google Play, Subscription required.

42. Tai Chi Foundation, taichifoundation.org, beginner to advanced, https://www.taichifoundation.org/live-online-courses/.

43. *Inside Bryson /DeChambeau's Brain Training* by Mike McAllister (2022), PGA, https://www.pgatour.com/article/news/long-form/2019/02/19/bryson-dechambeau-brain-training

44. *Breath: The New Science of a Lost Art*, James Nestor (2020), multiple references, https://www.penguinrandomhouse.com/books/547761/breath-by-james-nestor/.

45. Author's definition of Intuition.

46. *Trevino: An American Dream*, North Ridge Films (2024) Best Sports Documentary of the Year as voted by the Broadcast Sports Awards committee, https://northridgefilms.com/project—-trevino.html.

47. The Two Modes of an Athlete. The Dual-Process Theories in the field of Sport, Schweizer, G., & Bertrams, A., (2015), *International Review of Sport and Exercise Psychology*, 8(1), 106-124, https://www.researchgate.net/publication/271464131_The_two_modes_of_an_athlete_Dual-process_theories_in_the_field_of_sport.

48. Top Quotes: Flow: The Psychology of Optimal Experience (2023), https://peacejoyaustin.medium.com/top-quotes-flow-the-psychology-of-optimal-experience-mihaly-csikszentmihalyi-50c65046e4c5

49. *Flow: The Psychology of Optimal Experience* (1990), by Mihaly Csikszentmihalyi, chapter 2, https://www.harpercollins.com/products/flow-mihaly-csikszentmihalyi?variant=32118048686114.

50. *Flow: The Psychology of Optimal Experience* (1990), by Mihaly Csikszentmihalyi, page 40, https://www.harpercollins.com/products/flow-mihaly-csikszentmihalyi?variant=32118048686114.

51. *Flow: The Psychology of Optimal Experience* (1990), by Mihaly Csikszentmihalyi, multiple pages, https://www.harpercollins.com/products/flow-mihaly-csikszentmihalyi?variant=32118048686114

52. *A Tale of Two Coaches: Swing Coach vs Mental Golf Coach,*

Steven Yellin, website https://golfstateofmind.com/swing-coach-vs-mental-golf-coach/

53. Wulf, G. (2013). Attentional focus and motor learning: A review of 15 years. *International Review of Sport and Exercise Psychology*, 6(1), 77–104. https://gwulf.faculty.unlv.edu/wp-content/uploads/2018/11/Wulf_AF_review_2013.pdf

54. Wulf, G., et al. (2023). Golf skill learning: An external focus of attention enhances performance and motivation. *Psychology of Sport and Exercise*. https://pubmed.ncbi.nlm.nih.gov/37952707/

55. *The Inside Story of Matt Fitzpatrick's Dramatic Transformation*, Golf Digest (October, 2022) https://www.australiangolfdigest.com.au/cracking-the-code/

56. Comment by Sam Snead from Harvey Penick's Little Red Book (1992), page 37.

57. Tiger Woods demonstrating the magic of the transition, https://www.youtube.com/watch?v=R3jDc2eUepg

58. *The Golfing Machine: Geometric Golf: The Computer Age Approach to Golfing Perfection* Homer Kelley (1969), Edition 7.2, (2006), page XI.

59. *The Best Quotes of Tiger Woods*, from the blog majorcagolf.com, no date provided. https://majorcagolf.com/best-quotes-of-tigerwoods/.

60. *Perception, Cognition and Decision Training: The Quiet Eye in Action* (2007) by Dr. Joan Vickers. Also, from The Research Gate, https://www.researchgate.net/publication/369019654_Quiet_eye_training_alleviates_the_yips_in_golf_pu

61. *Harvey Penick's Little Red Book, Lessons and Teachings from a Lifetime in Golf* (1992), Harvey Penick with Bud Shrake, page 81.

Glossary

Alignment. The positioning of your body parallel to the target line. Part of the Core 4 setup fundamentals.

Analytical mind. The conscious, logical mode of thinking responsible for gathering information, making decisions, and preparing for each shot. Active during pre-shot routines and course management; should yield to the intuitive mind during execution.

Ball position. Where the ball sits relative to your stance—forward for drivers, center for irons. Part of the Core 4 setup fundamentals.

Basal ganglia. Brain structures that store and execute learned motor patterns below the level of conscious awareness. The neural home of your practiced golf swing.

Birdie conversion. The percentage of greens hit in regulation that result in birdies. A key performance indicator on the Flow Scorecard.

Carry distance. The distance a ball travels through the air before first hitting the ground, excluding roll. The most reliable number for club selection and course management.

Cognitive load. The mental energy consumed by unmade decisions, distractions, or disorganization. Reducing cognitive load frees the mind for present-moment awareness.

Commitment. The activation moment where mechanics, mindfulness, and intuition stop being separate elements and become one unified system. Not a thought—a mode switch from planning to doing.

Core 4. The four universal setup fundamentals that precede every shot: grip, posture, ball position, and alignment.

Course rating. A number representing the score a scratch golfer is expected to shoot under normal conditions, expressed as a decimal (e.g., 72.3). Measures overall course difficulty from a specific set of tees.

Declarative memory. The conscious memory system used for recalling facts, strategies, and decisions. Active during course management and pre-shot preparation. Compare with procedural memory.

Driving accuracy. The percentage of fairways hit on driving holes. A key performance indicator on the Flow Scorecard.

External focus. Directing attention toward the target or intended ball flight rather than toward body positions or swing mechanics. Research shows external focus produces better motor performance than internal focus.

Flow Index. A percentage calculated by dividing total Flow Score by total strokes for a round. Measures how consistently you accessed the integrated state where mechanics, mindfulness, and intuition worked together. A performance measure entirely under your control.

Flow Score. A post-shot assessment based on your pre-shot checklist. Each shot receives a score reflecting whether all checklist items were fully executed. Tracked by shot, hole, and round.

Flow Scorecard. A scoring system that captures traditional golf statistics alongside Flow Scores and the Flow Index, providing a complete picture of both mechanical and mental performance.

Flow state. A natural mental condition of complete absorption in an activity, characterized by effortless concentration, loss of self-consciousness, and altered perception of time. Identified by Dr. Mihaly Csikszentmihalyi.

GIR (green in regulation). Reaching the putting surface in the expected number of strokes—one stroke on a par 3, two on a par 4, three on a par 5. GIR percentage is a key performance indicator on the Flow Scorecard.

Grip. Your only physical connection to the club. The two most common grips are overlapping and interlocking. Part of the Core 4 setup fundamentals.

Grip pressure. The firmness with which you hold the club. Should be light enough to feel the grip texture but firm enough to maintain control.

Handicap stroke index. A ranking from 1 to 18 indicating where players receive handicap strokes on a course. The #1 hole isn't necessarily the hardest—it's where the scoring gap between low and high handicappers is greatest.

Intentional practice. A two-mode practice approach—swing mode and target mode—that brings mechanics, mindfulness, and intuition to every practice session, mirroring the demands of course play.

Internal par. A personal mental adjustment to a hole's difficulty based on your actual capabilities rather than the scorecard par. Reduces pressure and promotes better decision-making.

Intuitive mind. The subconscious mode of processing that understands feel, tempo, and pattern recognition without conscious reasoning. Responsible for executing the swing after the analytical mind completes preparation.

Mindfulness. Intentionally focusing attention on the present moment while calmly acknowledging thoughts and feelings without judgment. The discipline you cultivate; present-moment awareness is how you apply it on the course.

Motor memory. The neural patterns stored in brain circuits—including the basal ganglia, cerebellum, and motor cortex—that directly produce learned movements. Often incorrectly called "muscle memory." The motion is the memory.

Posture. Athletic body position at address—bending from the hips with slight knee flex, weight balanced over the balls of the feet. Part of the Core 4 setup fundamentals.

Pre-shot checklist. A personal list of three to five short, actionable items—both mechanical and mental—completed before each shot. When all items are checked, it signals the intuitive mind to take control. The basis for Flow Score assessment.

Present-moment awareness. The on-course application of mindfulness—being fully engaged with the current shot without dwelling on past results or anticipating future outcomes. Operates in two modes: open awareness and focused attention.

Procedural memory. The unconscious memory system that stores and executes learned motor skills, including your golf swing. Operates below awareness and doesn't require conscious supervision. Compare with declarative memory.

Quiet Eye. A visual technique identified by Dr. Joan Vickers in which the golfer maintains a steady gaze on the back of the ball for 2.5 to 3.0 seconds before initiating the swing. Promotes neural stability and supports intuitive execution.

Scrambling. Successfully completing a hole in par or better after missing the green in regulation, typically through a good chip or pitch followed by a one-putt. Scrambling percentage is a key performance indicator on the Flow Scorecard.

Slope rating. A number between 55 and 155 (113 is average) measuring how much harder a course plays for bogey golfers compared to scratch golfers. A higher slope means the course disproportionately challenges higher-handicap players.

State of Flow. See Flow state.

Swing mode. The first phase of intentional practice, focused on tempo and ball contact quality without concern for direction. Used for working on mechanics and building strike consistency.

Swing to Flow model. A three-element framework integrating mechanics, mindfulness, and intuition. When all three elements align, they create the conditions for peak golf performance through flow states.

Target mode. The second phase of intentional practice, focused on direction and simulating course play. Includes full pre-shot routines, commitment, and post-shot evaluation.

Tempo. The smooth, synchronized rhythm flowing from backswing through downswing. Not swing speed—players with different speeds can have equally good tempo. The soul of all good swings.

The Switch. The transition from analytical mind to intuitive mind during shot execution. The moment you stop planning and start trusting. The practical skill at the heart of the Swing to Flow process.

Up and down. Getting the ball into the hole in two strokes from off the green—typically one chip or pitch shot followed by one putt.

Visualization. Mentally rehearsing a shot before execution—seeing the ball flight, trajectory, and landing. An active, constructive practice that complements present-moment awareness.

About the Author

Steve Furman has played golf for fifty years. He's also spent thirty-five years practicing Buddhist meditation, earned a psychology degree, and led digital customer experience at a Fortune 500 company for two decades—where his job was understanding how people behave, make decisions, and navigate complexity. That combination led him to recognize something: golf instruction teaches mechanics brilliantly but doesn't show how mind and mechanics work together. This book bridges that gap.

Read more at swingtoflow.com.